Strand Bookstore
Poetry & More

Limited Edition 1 of 1

Poetry: The Patron Saint of Words

BOOKS BY THE AUTHOR

Red Lipstick & Stuck Piano Keys
Quiet Truth of History
Searching For a Shaman in a Land of Disbelief
Mardi Gras '97
Chipping Away at the Fossil Heart
This Tear: Is my Poem
Baby Sitting the Hearts of Women
Secret Life of a Deranged Poet
Mardi Gras 2000
Letters Never Written – A Poem not Read
New and Selected Poems 1984-2009
Sitting on Concrete - Ready to Saddle the Whirlwind
Church of the Backyard Fire
Du Beau Hostel – Arizona and Other Poems
Too Many Words About Nothing
    (Jawbone edition)
New York City Readings
Last Call to Escape Planet Earth
Film-Found Poems
Cleveland Hostel Poems
Poetry: The Tedious Mining of Words

Biography
Take Your Time But Hurry Up (Robert Collins)

Cleveland Anthology of Poets – 2007 Edition
Poems for People Who Hate Poetry – CD
The Big Uneasy – CD

Acknowledgments

Copyright 2014 Vladimir Swirynsky

Greatful acknowledgment is made to the editors of the followning publications where these poems first appeared.

Alembic: "March 25, 1911"; *Artisan-A-Journal Of Craft:* "New Mexico Bus Blues"*; Avatar Review:* "Sacred Links, Hiding in our Own Skins";*Blast Furnace "The Forbidden Herb of Love'; California Quarterly*: "Images"; *Camrock Press Review* "Impoverished, Already the Sky on Bended Knees"; *Clark Street Review, Doubting Thomas, Ellipsis:* **(Westminster College)** "Lit Cigarette In The Night"; **Footprint:** "Water"; *Gemini Magazine "Venice Beach"; Glass Tesseract: "*Mardi Gras '97 The Struggle"*; Hessler Street Fair Anthology*: "Already The Sky on Bent Knees" **first place winner.** *The Iconoclast:* "Lowell Observatory"; *Jawbone 2000, Lynx Eye:* "Boston"*; Mobius, The Poetry Magazine*: "Thunder"; *Mojo Risin*: "West 98th Stret"; *OMNIFIC:* "If Ever I Should Die"*; The Poet's Den:* "Stagecoach"; *Poetic License; Portland Review* "Wheat for Bread"; *Stepping Stones Magazine*: "Coal Mine"; *Sunflower Dream, Thought Magazine*: "Deep Tracks of Snow"; *Yefief:* "Oh Jerusalem".

Front cover: oil on Canvas by Maria Winarski

"This Tear Is My Poem" published by Implosion Press copyright 2002. Special thanks to the following people who contributed their time and talents in making this book possible: *Art Berg, Maria Winarski, Cheryl Townsend, Sharlene & Eckhart, Rodney Mapes and especially Susan Hassenzalh Swirynsky*

Light Omens: An introduction/testimony for Vlad
by RA Washington

"That night...this night
we are with strangers, holding hands
The impossible dream raging in the flames of candles
Sometimes there's no excape from this city."

Poets are hard, they are always looking around, shifting, recording. There is also madness, and glee. All the light and dark of a world populated by upright animals. Its a sacred calling- Poet, and it is also shameful, replete with tiny cuts, wounds recorded in meter, in the celibate line.

I was only 17 when I first met/heard Vladimir Swirynsky. It was a strange singing, so honest, odd, limping and at the same time it was royal. Epic. Human. There were characters I recognized (even at the young age) villains I had never fathomed. I was awestruck by the lack of applause, at the fearful looks until another older man, who always went to see poetry said,

"Its because they are afraid."

I had no concept for it. It was like being drunk for the first time. The euphoric rush, followed by the grief that it was all over. Vladimir's poems our time capsules, snapshots of us failing and loving and dying. There is a voice present in his work, but it never yells "LOOK AT ME". The voice hides, and shifts. It is an omen, and a testimony. We wish for you to leave this book with your heart and mind blown away by its beauty and splendor, we wish for you to leave this earth remembering that once, years before this- (your final breath)- you took a chance on an unknown poet, and came away singing his name.

Poetry: The Patron Saint of Words

New & Collected Works
by Vladimir Swirynsky

Front Cover
Painting by **Maria Winarski**

New Kiev Publishing

This Tear: Is my Poem

Mardi Gras 2000

Last Call To Escape Planet Earth

Last Call to Escape Planet Earth

New Poems

If you want a miracle
you'll have to wait in a long
line, God's busy tidying
up his modest studio.

AVE MARIA

(for Maria Winiarski)

You and your mother browse in the market, these beloved scrap iron streets of Krakow that mostly offer; one item – one size Thank God most of us survived those turn of the century madmen In that rare moment when you find oranges or raisins for sale the world breaks open like a fortune cookie Every time someone moves a black or white pawn you feel the peace of Christ Strangers buy you lody just to have a moment or a few words with your mom you listen to the sweet voice of the caterpillar, each of you desire open fields, your eyes pleading, *show me the world...show me a piece of it* Discouraged from reading, not allowed to smile or laugh you slow dance with agony while waiting for your breasts The tug-of-war, that constant bickering forces you to sneak out at night, the moon like black wings, your younger sister's smile What was missing was love—Your door cracked open to listen, the men drunk as they retold stories about the war, how the Nazi's picked up men at random, stringing them up, using two by fours to get confessions and useless information Your uncle Ludwig the only saving grace...Polish pilot, an artist who flew for the RAF You adored him He'd bring chocolate from Switzerland Up early you would spy on him as he would be getting dressed It was his Java motorcycle that excited you, riding in the sidecar through town He was so brave, you were so young, your heart knowing he alone was saving the world Sweet child how could you not adore him All too soon you discover how quickly the world can crush us The cicadas quiet, comes the news of his death in a crash You cry, try to be a noble angel In the end you save a tear and wrap it in burlap I rescue you only now, unwrap your soul to find that precious tear

9

There were hills—It was a raw blue night—the stars in flannel
shirts   A beautiful horse running, running past the herd   Then
he stopped for me   He told me Get Free!   stay free
I offered him a silver apple but he wouldn't let me ride him

The painter's first loyalty is to the canvas,
Not to the outside world

I am a child with water colors painting a yellow
sun so big it melts away all the bad memories,
the torture of my violin lessons
Reduces to nothing my Halloween wax lips on the sidewalk
A wash of crimson darkens the surface—
A wild country
I've been wanting to call earth
(So long ago I created this moment in the sun)

I am invincible…lonely
Forever twenty-two, shirt off
Watching them tear down the Stardust Drive-In
Three days into summer and already
I'm putting bridal gowns on my Barbie dolls
I feel this sensation of being lost in a crowd, on the
street I shout out; *your beauty cannot be exaggerated*
We are in the same city but why can't I find you?
I am twenty-two, In Vietnam smoking weed,
the clouds barefoot travelers
and you are a pebble here and there

I mailed out a nickel post card It reads; I'm not the first
to tell you that nothing lasts forever, only the dead are lucky
Today you tell me you want the *Real Thing,*
that you need more lovers
I tell you that we are living the same story,
afraid of the same things
Together we place a penny in the gumball machine
What drops out is a dark morning,
you say; it's the eye of the black bird

In my dream your cat
and I take turns sleeping on the couch
With a little coaxing he shares your secrets
"Ask her about Picasso, she will read out of
a white book and tell you all about Picasso"
Like the priests I hide my collar to shield my
ignorance of art   Once...it took years to circle the
globe...the women would wait   It is only a matter
of time before you rush to my door not knowing why
I bow to the genius of Picasso, study the work
from his blue period   I absorb the birth
of this modern abstraction movement
Shamed by my casual ignorance   I feel my manhood
being disfigured, it has turned into a Picasso fish,
I wrap A towel around it, hope the gods forgive me
(this a punishment for my blind arrogance)
How can I make love to you now?

Who were those fools
who tried to climb the highest mountainsfor you?
I've bought all the red lipstick at the cosmetic counter
Signed my unemployment check in blood red
What if I kiss you, what if all the fruit
falls off the tree, will you kiss me then?
You're reading the paper, your tears
islands of disbelief, I say, "I hope someone
finds all those lost pets"   I admire the poppy's
in your garden, half-expecting you to lay a baby
down in your flower bed so it may fall asleep
On the couch I stroke your hair
"Women need to make money, all artist
suffer"...you say   I open all the windows,
look at you—

there's a salesman at the door,
coins falling out of my pocket
So we curse the spiteful sky, dance
the night 'til I offer you my mutilated body
You tell Edward Hopper
to leave us alone
Some shadow in the room becomes
a song, a souvenir,
an object of our affection

You...who taught me everything
I'm setting a table for two in Hell's Kitchen
Will you join me?
I'll bring flowers, my two left feet
Having seduced the messenger
you must know that the sun is in Scorpio,
Venus is the fire
Tomorrow as you awake reaching for
Your first cigarette
Maria—
As you're taking your second breath
I've already made love to you

AVE—

SAXOPHONE MAN
for Rodney Mapes

Saxophone man,
every five minutes I call the operator, they
keep telling me that love is an unlisted number
Saxophone man, first time I heard
you play, your guts were puking out midnight
An ugly frog in the gutter telling you;
 don't count your chickens before they hatch
It makes sense now, long time ago black,
forever 103rd street—Bank shot,
two ball in the corner pocket - John Coltrane
 throws a five spot on the table and leaves
I look Billie Holiday straight in the eye
and say, do something to me
Let me be your pusher, your pimp
I promise, you won't ever have to sing the
blues for them to call you, *lady*
Saxophone man, you drink too much,
everybody tells you that Last night we got
high, driving on the freeway you were
singing the *Battle Hymn Of The Republic*
while I pretended to be a tuba, almost happy
I'm tired of all the company that comes
over begging you to perform
Is it true you soak your reed in whiskey?

Saxophone man, this is all new to me
I'm drinking lots of booze, listening
to electric guitars and drums
There's a propellor hanging on the wall
Honest, a mermaid was sitting at the bar,
she gave me her diamond earrings
Saxophone man,
I don't know where you are, but I am alive
with the night and I'm stealing your woman
Walk barefoot she does, a white canvas
that sticks her tongue out at the world
She says you're a genuis
but you won't make love to her
At the kitchen table we keep our eye
on the Trojan horse and her
sun fire tomatoes
The only notes left in your sax barely
wail out, *baby*
Whatever breath left, is a quiet rage,
a sweet mercy that dances in a dark alley
Saxophone man, I'm running out of roses
to fill these empty wine bottles
Before you paint the swan black
Before your poison destroys me
I'm gonna run outside,
telling the first woman I meet
I know you want to make love to me
and I'm ready

IN THE DARK HOURS

Post war America,
rich top soil falls prey to silent auctions
Look at the faces of the sharecropers,
the sign that reads; *Chesterfields satisfy*,
all this and more lost in the immensity
of the dead end moon
Some embraced the believable lies,
headed for California to pick
peas for a penny a pound
Those left behind in the scorching heat
found it hard to listen to the preachers
They put their faith in the blues,
 swaying to love's own beat
An occasional photographer
would pass by and take notice
Bless them indeed for allowing
us to see the stark beauty of human erosion
Beneath the bone some crazy courage
enabled them to laugh at the sight of what
must of seemed like endless rows of cotton,
hardships—
The poem comes in the moment,
believes in Texas rain, that the sun
is nothing more than a black pearl
The wind easeful colorful banners,
a gentle scattering of voices

The poem comes in the moment,
believes in Texas rain, that the sun
is nothing more than a black pearl
The wind easeful colorful banners,
a gentle scattering of voices

We crave for the simple things in life,
a triumphant blue sky,
parades with beautiful women on stilts
Gazing at the horizon we bite
into ten cents worth of memory
All that hard work and no closer to the stars
So we retreat to our childhood dreams
We hear a voice, *grab yourself a cold soda*
Holding the bottle like rare earth,
for once offer the legion
of gods not a drop

I AM THINKING KITTENS

The sun is out...but it warms nothing
The universe an endless sidewalk sale and I'm
cutting out a coupon to save 59 cents on toilet paper
Glen Miller's *Is you is or is you ain't my baby?*
surges on mystic wings through the open window
kicking me in the behind like an Irish Jig
The sun is out and I am thinking kittens, Canasta,
sleepovers and pillow fights
I love the cheap thrills of going through life's toy box
My wife promised to read me a Dr. Seuss story
I am a lucky man

Key turns, lights flicker - I am open for business
Ready for the misfortune that walks through the door
Bill is outside, waiting, his bohemian soul
lost, without a kickstand like his bicycle
His wife dead from cancer
He is drunk, his brilliant mind snuffed out long ago
His treasures from the attic are more like
the rubbish people throw out on collection day
Smokes his camels and praises the virtues of cigars
Yells; Damn the prostitutes they take all my money

I am trying to save him from himself
He is a squirrel crossing an L.A. freeway at rush hour
Sits on the roof and swears that the stars
move slower than molasses
If you divide the day into hours you are doomed

He curses the genius of Beethoven
Old man! Is it true you were caught shoplifting
from the store across the street?
Are you the forgotten Samurai of Joe
DiMaggio laying a red rose on Marilyn's grave
He takes another puff, shouts;
I don't give a damn if the women are ugly,
as long as they wear tight corduroys

It's getting late
He borrows a dollar
Next door the fortune tellers are twisting
off bottle caps in hopes of finding a winner
Jupiter is rising
There is bloodshed in the holy lands
It never seems to end
The plants in the store are dying
Yes I am still thinking kittens
I will not water the plants
I will not!
It is better that way

DEEP TRACKS OF SNOW

In the work camps you become a Buddha,
a good luck charm embracing
the rewards of hardship
There is ample time for rediscovery,
for the body to become a replica of death
Give me the high-strung eyes of Rasputin,
his fertile mind of insanity
I am fireweed—
ready to endure two Russian winters
To enjoy the glory of being laid to rest
with a full beard like his
But first, send me a princess who's
not afraid to wear a man's muddy black boots
Put her on a train to Siberia with my photograph
She will see misery, the eyes of old men
shouting out for death
This is the rose I offer her
I will tell her she is Sylvia Plath
That we are safe at the Coney Island fun house,
far from the reaches of tyranny In this frozen
tundra my heart has turned into root,
therefore; I am neither man or stone
I am a closed eye,
a prehistoric woolly mammoth to be dug up,
a meal for the czar She on the other hand
points at every nervous ghost
But I see nothing, only hear
the loud noise of celebrations,
the endless serenade of revolution

Lenin is packing his old brown suitcase,
a Punch and Judy showman,
a scholar who raised a new flag,
lecturing wearing the only tie he ever owned,
(as always his foot on the neck of a beautiful swan)
who best to teach us despair,
the promise of nothing,
this half-heart of doubt finally removed
by your touch of unexpected mercy
Outside self proclaimed holy men are
as mute as grazing cows
The wolves nothing more
than the shadows of heaven
From the shallow graves of death camps,
root and rock whisper
We survive, forgive,
thumb prints of hope that
continue to love for no good reason

THE UNEASY STREETS

Late November
     The times they are a changin'
The flags still faithful to the wind
Latin soul, Count Basie settin' the woods on fire
T-bone Walker, the windshield wipers
and I trying to find a blue note lost----
     That night...this night
There's anarchy, mischief galore in the passing
lanes and my turn signals aren't working
Warehouses full of nursery rhymes for a
small planet but the dock workers are on strike
Black crows and the Prince of Darkness
now the watershed of winter sonnets
     Tickets in hand - we notice the sign
Please hold the hand rail
     We look around suspiciously
The Blue Line - Franconia/Spring Station
Train approaching...arriving
White lights flashing on the platform
     Doors open...close - open
I snap my fingers but it's still out there,
the crowds bigger, angrier
Poets taking aim at dead center
The homeless who curse God but praise hunger
continue their jubilee, the quest for quarters -
This plankton that the soul requires

That night...this night
we are with strangers, holding hands
The impossible dream raging in the flames of candles
A storm of forgiveness we call My Sweet Lord
Sometimes there's no escape from this city
King Kong tried, climbed as high as he could---
was shot dead and fell into our hearts
We rush past, unnoticed
Hoping to trip over a small miracle
But all we get is more of the same
A blind Buddha telling us to keep the faith
Boxcar Willie trying to sing the blues
That beatnik Ginsberg forever sticking his nose
where it doesn't belong, standing on a stone
statue and giving everyone the finger---asking,
Why are there no Negroes around
I walk over to a woman seated on a
park bench, hand her my torn jacket
Tell her this is Walt Whitman's America
Sometimes the city cuddles into our arms
like a shoebox full of dreams, a lost love
or postcards from Africa that bring the
world that much closer to our souls
There's a knock at the door
I'm expecting brick oven pizza, instead I get
the skin and bones of a Woody Allen film
I prefer Paris after dark or a matinee showing of
Dr. Strangeglove or how I learned
to love the bomb

I recall my friend who perched himself
on the 10th floor convinced he could find
a shortcut to heaven
Who once said,
If you put chalk in the hands of a child
they will write on the sidewalk
"To my best pal I ever had
I'm sorry I did you wrong"
Comes nightfall, the cold breath of our honesty
 rises into the darkness to become a lost object
We are permitted to search
Never to discover what it was

AFTERMATH: SUMMER 1972

All my friends thought poetry was just
words, useless, a jealous discipline
that didn't even have a birth certificate
Poetry was inane as a goat in a gilded tree
I was still jumping barbed wire fences
Getting ready for water balloon fights
Children starving in China, pop art,
The war in Vietnam, arson in the ghetto
falling at the feet of Napoleon   Violence
glorified, we toasted our impending doom

Headline

37 who saw murder didn't call police
Apathy at stabbing of Queens
woman shocks inspector
Her voice crying out, crying out for help
We shut our windows, raised the volume
on our radios and televisions   The next
morning the summer heat returns and
we are blessed with short memories
But there is no escape from
misery for any of us,
      ever

THE LAST LEAF

The endless summer is no more
The bridge freshly painted tightfisted black
All we have is a slingshot to rid
the world of geese As they fly overhead
in search of ancient woodlands
What purpose the wind but to free the last leaf
and send it spinning to some random point
The rings in the tree, think of them
as a large vinyl record,
a foray into the boring medley of history
It's true, we showcase our hardships, pile
rock on rock into this self professed anthology
Who's to say the universe is endless
That faith is the untouched food of the soul
At home the phone rings off the hook from
frantic friends who have no lovers
The seasons out of cadence, our life, if you
please like a rolled up poster No wonder
the world drifts away from us as though
behind our ugly faces was even an uglier face
We allow the sun to vanish
Telling each other about the hungry wolf
Yet unsure of all the details
The darkness, the universe whispers
All we hear is the awkward silence
But who in this bed already
hears the birds of the morning?

SUGARCOATED

(for Jennifer Napier)

We chose the café Noir to meet
You and your amazing sidekick
(the human map) got lost, never showed up
The next day you bought me coffee at Borders
My life story told in about five words
and six short hours of laughter
So much can happen in a conversation
Our birthdays were two days apart
Jokingly I said you could be my birthday
present, the twenty-seven year old woman
I always wanted You sat there like a bare
Christmas tree that everyone wanted
to decorate You were my Autumn Sojourn,
a young Marianne Moore,
A canary gently placed inside a small cage
We went out for a smoke in the cold
and shivered like love-struck teenagers
We are poets not refrigerator magnets
We are poets not men and women
We are poets! I underline those words,
I tear up the paper, crumple it up into a ball
and let it sit on the desk telling myself
I do not feel vulnerable
There are things beyond our control
Is everything within our reach poison?
I bury myself in the pages of Elizabeth Bishop
and I am the Armadillo
The snow is starting to fall and I feel safe

I look out the window again and find
myself crying for a newborn infant
The piano out of tune and every ivory key
looks like a swollen tongue Before I go on,
if the spring flowers are to bloom,
if the neighbors are to think that I'm crazy,
I must pick up the fiddle, rosin up the bow,
turn the car's headlights, dance out in the cold
This is a celebration for the world,
for the impoverished
The snow flakes are large and wet, so what
if I never owned a sled
This strange fragrance of poem on page doesn't
have a name yet but the beauty mark
a stroke of genius My chair is next to her's now
I've gotten so close we find ourselves in a chapel
The snow piled high against the door
I am wearing a button that says, *Bomb Hanoi*
I've abandoned everything Even your journal
mentions of a forbidden city
A Mayan reference to the end of the world
The universe is already in shambles
The blizzard sugar coated, a backwash
of mischief—It's now or never
you spread your wings to scare me off
But it's too late I'm no longer a stranger
You see it in my eyes
I would die if I could touch your long hair

OH JERUSALEM

You are hostage to the rumors of peace
Afraid to open the book of blessings
Nothing around but the scorched earth to kiss
You have see everything
Yet, hear nothing but the breaking of bones
Touch the skin, this fortress of verse
Rest here at the water's edge,
if only for a moment You carry a hatred
that has no face, that has escaped
every prison cell This has become your place
in the sun-a slow orbit of memory,
a sky so peaceful how could it not unfold
and touch everything below
You have returned to nowhere
      Wearing the uniform of sadness
Your death already rehearsed
Sharing kinship with those souls
shouting from the rooftops
      It is the beginning of the end
Avoid the marketplace, the crowded streets
      Beat the innocent until
the suspected confesses

Each stone you pick up is a stanza of joy
Your aim guided by the death of your mother
All along the watchtower the password is...
Save us Mr. Bojangles
In the healing garden you teach your younger
sisters how to add and subtract with clenched fists
Beat the innocent until
the suspect confesses
A mask covers your face, the tears, the
tenderness of grief that seems so abstract
You spit at the face of those who are hostage
to a God who was crucified and died in
these same holy lands
You will inherit nothing but the stories
told to your father by his father
Lynched because you are a Jew
Lynched because you are an Arab
Slapped because you dare to utter
a word in prayer or protest
Killings...Killings...Killings
Oh City of Jerusalem! this love
will destroy us all
Hear me, we are nothing but borrowers of tragedy
Children dig in the ruins, searching for songs,
out of colorful illustrations reconstruct
the legendary bird of prey
I hear Credance Clearwater Revival singing,
who'll stop the rain

I saw a soldier step on the Koran
Olive trees uprooted for roads, settlements
Drunken men blasting the ram's horn, trying
to make sense of what they were feeling
      Before Islam,
      before Christianity,
      before the imprint of rulers on gold coins
      there was one over riding doctrine
        Might makes right—
There is no street named mercy, no poster
to be found of Gandhi fasting
Who among us is the oppressor laughing?
      We have peace on paper
        We are left with bloodshed   .
      We have a handshake
        We are left with bloodshed
      We have a piece of paper
        We are left with bloodshed
Someone cries out in the night
We have the scriptures
The morning sun takes pleasure
in our earthly hunger's,
      and they beat the suspect until
        there is nothing left to confess,
         nothing left to love

WEST 98TH & LORAIN AVENUE

Richard Nixon, you'll always be our China Doll
You have the honors to drop the bomb...sir
I am furious at the young girl next door that's pregnant
My neighbors are so savvy, they steal and
shoot hoops in the back yard
They tell me, go ahead...work for the better life
Why is it I'm disappointed in all my friends?
Arms for hostages, the tentacles of New Age,
Eleven o'clock check out, tell me dreamboy, why do
I worship this sizzle-spit world?
I've interviewed many eyewitnesses, they all
say I'm a whiz at bumming cigarettes
I am afraid to offer the prostitute twenty dollars
She is barefoot, a noticeable beauty mark on her leg
A large purse that's more like a P.O. box
I know what she can offer---
A soul embarking on another trip into the abyss
On this hot summer day middle aged men hang
out the open windows
Their large bellies like silent drums
At the B & J Restaurant the cook is a meek soul
She knows the world and it offers her very little, I admire her
I want to meet that fellow that called me a genius
Why did I ever leave that woman who had plenty of
time and was willing to listen to my fantasies?
I want to look into the mirror and be surprised,
To see that I'm clean shaven

POEM INSPIRED
BY THREE WOMEN

You called early in the morning
Said you were depressed,
hadn't written a word
Everything I've written lately is like
broken glass, something to be swept away
I want the words, *pretty baby* to undress me
Mademoiselle—
please forgive me,
we are all blameless
I for one stumble in and out of my poems
Haunted by ex-lovers, it is the sun I
worship now, asking strangers
for permission to cross the street
Last time I was in northern Arizona
the snow felt like warm rain
Even the priests are sinning
I am sending you a gift,
the mirror off my car
I am bringing my camera
Once we stopped to have my fortune told
I watched the old woman open up
her bag of bone
Felt the presence of JuJu Man
Her face turning into an ancient clock

That evening you were chopping carrots,
making soup
You called to say you were on fire
This time I didn't look both ways
I had no name, everything else forgotten
Something about your lips,
like a flash of legs
Your sharp tongue like a white girl's
cotton skirt, backseat curlique,
12:42PM, last pizza delivered,
cigarette hanging out of your mouth,
you smile: *Give it to me!*
I was an old poet, a charred soldier,
this was oblivion
All in all a night of hard love
Daybreak rattles across your ribs
If I touch you now—
what will my punishment be?

DEAREST MOM

1.

You are washing dishes, I'm seventeen, my
arms around you as I kiss you on the cheek
    I love you mom
For our own good, memory and photographs fade,
those things we hid under the sofa cushion
are but a gentle passing of summer
You pleaded with us to behave
All we managed to do was make a mockery
of the old country, the old ways
What did we know of love?
We barely followed the ten commandments
I am sorry I didn't wear my Army uniform for
you when we went to church that Sunday

2.

Only now am I aware of the masterpiece
which was your heart, your love---
The world was a horror, I saved my pennies,
never enough to buy you a new dress
Yeats wrote of *The Pilgrim Soul*
On your mother's day card I wrote something
sweet, it brought a smile to our faces
That is where the poem begins...ends
I have planted a garden of flowers and a packet
of radishes to teach me the grammar of silence
Your courage allowing me to dance with strangers
The gift of forgiveness ignites into flames,
falls like rain becoming a river of slow belief

3.

Your picture hangs on the wall
I've looked into those dark eyes and
swear sometimes I see a Jewish cemetery,
feel a sadness older than the flesh
My name is first born
Look through me, see your granddaughter that
was hiding in a belly when you passed away
What can I tell you dearest mother
To read out of the Sears & Roebuck Catalogue
I discarded the mother tongue
That the London Bridge is in Arizona
My hair is growing longer, I hope you approve
There is so much to tell you

4.

Ask my heart what it remembers, ask me if I cried
I am angry, crying because I should
have married a Polish or Ukrainian woman
I treasure those moments when you counted on
me to be a man, to help drag dad into the house
I still laugh at the flat-out mayhem your
broken English caused at the food markets
I've given up on saving my own soul, my heart,
the wild wind now belong to Venus de Milo
I am lost - but lost in a good sense
a stranger even you wouldn't open the door for
My only comforts, a bamboo back scratcher
and my little bell that I sometimes ring
Never a day I don't think of you

5.

I've made my offerings in a wooden church called
Crazy Louie's pawn shop, spent a week staying
over at Jack Keourac's house in Orlando
The drawbridge down, from a small cafe I look
up at the full moon over Miami Beach
Listen to Spanish love songs on the radio
I think of Jackie Gleason
      One of these days Alice, to the moon
We did, just a few years later and up the road a little
Frightened and in awe, more determined than
ever to worship the God of my choice
I light a candle and place it on the skull of an alligator
My heart becomes a glass eye that forever
will mistake the blue sky for a perfect love

6.

It's all here in the brochure, the pages
of a bedtime story turned by the unseen hand
Children gathering up crows feet, tongues of the
dead in the wicked forest
1100 scenic miles inside a box car
      Clank - Clang - Clack
    Clank - Clang - Clack
Never to see your family again
How much of eternity did you endure
convinced that the war would never end?

7.

Who is it that is sending me these dreams?
I am trying to ignore the comings and goings of
thousands of women digging trenches for the Nazis
I step on a mouse but it is only a sock
I keep hearing rifle shots, bombs exploding,
people crying out the name of loved ones
All this orchestrated by the high priest of hatred
With no identification or food where could they go?
Love, the only song that offers us hope
Someone pushes a small piece of bread
through the fence, is that you mother?

8.

The past, present, future have come together here
at Webster Flea Market   I hear the rhythm,
noise of fresh pecans being cracked by a machine
    Clank - Clang - Clack
    Clank - Clang - Clack
I am crossing into the unknown, rushing toward
the guns, almost at the birthplace of your fears
The earth is unaware of the beating drums
In the darkness I trip over the half-buried,
they remind me that the truth must survive
On the ground a pocket mirror swallowing itself,
what word disappears, what plague to replace it
Mom—I would visit more often
but I don't know what to say

BEAUTY

In Willis O'Brien's
epic and unforgettable
motion picture
King Kong
It wasn't beauty
that killed the beast
It was
Hollywood

MONDAY

I am paranoid
Unwilling to emerge from my hiding place
My tongue caught in a zipper
Worried how to start, how to end this poem
I am looking forward to Thursday, a woman
will kiss me for three and a half seconds
It's not what you think---
I want to teach myself discipline,
to respond to the perfume of words
It's more about the voice, not the art
It's more about letting your insanity out,
not keeping it in
I'm not sure of the meaning of contemporary
Am I a part of the definition?
I'm beginning to understand sexually explicit art,
although I lack the courage to enjoy it
It is Monday, my best day, my only
day for writing
I have a fixation for the misery of others
I hang up on answering machines
Wander from gallery to gallery offering
up my poems like a good country doctor
It's almost midnight,
Blind Willie Johnson nudges me to sleep
My shirt folded neatly
The missing button without a
prayer of changing the world

LATE NIGHT RADIO

This new generation of poets is sophisticated,
angry—
dredging deep into the psyche of human debris
I say it's not enough to be faithful to our craft,
High time we got out of Gotham City,
out of the pages of our own misery
I'm fighting back by having fun, laughing
(fearing nothing except beauty)
Listening to late night radio

2AM, Radio on...live, without a safety net
the world comes out of hiding
The energizer bunny quietly
sneaking behind enemy lines
Sink or swim a first time caller from Virginia
swears Francis Gary Powers just
parachuted into her vegetable patch
          (there goes the eggplant parmesan)
Things are what they are...
The static, the signals bleeding in,
are they the Ten Lost Tribes?
Peoples of the third world crying out that
they hear the footsteps of Armageddon
Bulldozers, tanks knocking down
the walls of Jericho

2:18, a twelve year old calls in to explain
quantum mechanics and why girls are so icky
White substance, chem trails falling from the sky
Something's going on, but what?

Change is continuous, nothing truly random
2:44, report of cattle mutilations...a disconnect
hello...hello, caller, are you there?
Keep searching, it's somewhere on the dial
a steady diet of make believe stories,
a cousin in Boise who doesn't
know what country she's living in
That two out of three Elvis impersonators
are actually Liberace
The world has no small problems,
a fourteen year old calls in, says
she's possessed by Britney Spears

Almost Daybreak---my call goes through
hello; listen... at the Brecksville VA Hospital
they keep showing over and over
"One Flew Over The Cuckoos Nest"
They read the Sunday comics out loud—
nobody laughs
The hell with changing their bed pans
let them smoke Marijuana,
give them X-rated videos
          ...save a bullet for me

The static returns, I catch a word
or two about crop circles
More static, the words barely audible
          "Gort, Klaatu Barada Nikto"
Something's going on, but what?

K.K.K. RALLY

Pick a day in August, a Saturday
afternoon will do
Put up green fluorescent signs
Maybe they should read---
         Entry for opponents of k.k.k .rally
         Entry for supporters of k.k.k. rally
Barricade the streets, remove all
the newsstands and bus shelters
Block the alleys to the library and
courthouse with chain link fences
Notify the public they are subject
to a physical search
Make sure everyone walks
through the metal detectors
Throw in the mounted police to
give anarchy some character
If you truly have patience,
try to find compassion or love
somewhere in this photo on the front page
         A City shut down by a few men
         who have nothing of worth to say
         Peeking out into this world
         through slits cut in their souls---

WAITING FOR THE PARADE

Canal street, New Orleans police barricade
the road, tell us if we cross over to the other
side of the rope they will arrest us A young man,
drunk, is passed out on the curb face up
A vendor says; looks like the hurricanes got him
Some kids come over and decide to have some fun
by putting cigarettes up his nose and ear
They tie his shoe strings together and place a
Domino's pizza box over him like a blanket
I turn around and tell the crowd,
"we don't even know his name"
People across the street see all the commotion
and run over with their cameras, snap pictures
I feel sorry for him, a sense
of bewilderment reflects off the glass buildings
These shiny beads we wear are nothing
more than a celebration of our frailties
Some of us will leave disappointed
by our lack of courage
Disappointed that Mardi Gras will
never be as magical as a loving hug,
        or...thinking about your wife,
who's a thousand miles away

UNTITLED POEM

Like every good poet there is a part of me that is a
flower,
a thought that struggles to get by on a wooden leg
I bide my time, reel in small catches of childhood memories
Sitting at the same table for two by the fireplace and
lamenting the anarchy of our yesterdays
The women who come and go that we never speak to
All the waiting---
       the view out the window, the horrible silence,
       the bare trees, the slush
There are days I throw small pebbles to recall a word
The discipline extracting a heavy toll
The poem like an anxious bride,
a beauty to be sold at the slave market
It's not enough to be faithful to our craft
Art is Art is absolute !PARC
Only the great poets wear Sergio Valente jeans
and demand the power of X
Only the great poets achieve immortality
       Out of the clear blue---
       like someone in love, they
       anoint the page with bedlam
I am not writing for the children of Prague
Have not, as yet, written about apricots or dragonflies
I am a poor vagabond forced to admit that
the cash register is our greatest enemy
      Stuck between sea and sky
I continue to wait for someone
who will never show up

CONVERSATION

It's a short trip on Arthur's bicycle,
four mail boxes down then a sharp right turn
onto a bumpy dirt road
Back by the pond a campfire dark-soiled
with large red embers, thousands
of azaleas standing guard Looks like
like the boys were here, Rolling Rock
beer bottles proudly scattered all around
I pick up a plastic fork and knife off
the ground and cut little squres of wet moss,
toss them into the fire and watch the white
smoke rise Somewhre deeper in the woods
are the wars we never won,
the battles we were unwilling to fight
I picture my first love in a yellow dress,
a swing that barely extends over the water
It was here I over came my fears
and swung close to the edge
of the water line and let go
I realize the world and I are in need,
all of us pleading for a long kiss
I yell out for cupid to let his arrows fly
Then quietly sit on a stump and start up
a conversation as though every tree had
a name, a sad story to share with me

Susan, I love you, Susan, I love you, Susan, I love you, SUSAN
I LOVEYOU SUSAN I LOVEYOU SUSAN I LOVEYOU SUSAN I LOVEYOU SUSAN
Susan, I love you, Susan, I love you, Susan, I love you, SUSAN
I LOVEYOU SUSAN I LOVEYOU SUSAN I LOVEYOU SUSAN I LOVEYOU SUSAN
SUSAN, I LOVE YOU SUSAN I LOVE YOU SUSAN, I LOVE YOU
I LOVEY OUSUSAN I LOVEYOU
Susan, n, I love you, SUSAN
I LOVEY SAN I LOVEYOU SUSAN
SUSAN SUSAN, I LOVE YOU
I LOVEY OUSUSAN I LOVEYOU
Susan, I n, I love you, SUSAN
I LOVEYOU SUSAN I LOVEYOU SUSAN
SUSAN, I LO OU SUSAN, I LOVE YOU I
LOVEYOUSUS OVEYOUSUSAN I LOVEYOU
Susan, I love yo u, Susan, I love you, SUSAN
I LOVEYOU SUSAN I B OVEYOU SUSAN I LOVEYOU SUSAN
SUSAN, I LOVE YO LOVE YOU SUSAN, I LOVE YOU I
LOVEYOUSUSAN I LO SAN I LOVEYOUSUSAN I LOVEYOU
Susan, I love you, Sus love you, Susan, I love you, SUSAN
I LOVEYOU SUSAN I LOVEYO USAN I LOVEYOU SUSAN I LOVEYOU SUSAN
SUSAN, I LOVE YOU SUSAN, I LOVE YOU SUSAN, I LOVE YOU
I LOVEYOUSUSAN I LOVEYOUSUSAN I LOVEYOUSUSAN I LOVEYOU
Susan, I love you, Susan, I love you, Susan, I love you, SUSAN
I LOVEYOU SUSAN I LOVEYOU SUSAN I LOVEYOU SUSAN I LOVEYOU SUSAN
SUSAN, I LOVE YOU SUSAN, I LOVE YOU SUSAN, I LOVE YOU
I LOVEYOUSUSAN I LOVEYOUSUSAN I LOVEYOUSUSAN I LOVEYOU
Susan, I love you, Susan, I love you, Susan, I love you, SUSAN
I LOVEYOU SUSAN I LOVEYOU SUSAN I LOVEYOU SUSAN I LOVEYOU SUSAN
SUSAN, I LOVE YOU SUSAN, I L OU SUS I LOVE YOU
I LOVEYOU SUSAN I LOVEYOUSU EY LOVEYOU
Susan, I love you, Susan, I lo u, SUSAN
I LOVEYOU SUSAN I LOVEYOU SU DU SUSAN
SUSAN, I LOVE YOU SUSAN, I OVE YOU
I LOVEYOUSUSAN I LOVEYOUSU I LOVEYOU
SUSAN, I LOVE YOU SUSAN, I LO , I LOVE YOU
I LOVEYOUSUSAN I LOVEYOUSUSAN USAN I LOVEYOU
SUSAN, I LOVE YOU SUSAN, I LOVE SAN, I LOVE YOU
I LOVEYOUSUSAN I LOVEYOUSUSAN I LO USUSAN I LOVEYOU
Susan, I love you, Susan, I love you, Sus n, I love you, SUSAN
I LOVEYOU AN VEYOU SUSAN I LOVEYOU SUSAN I LOVEYOU SUSAN
SUSAN, SUSAN I LOVEYOU SUSAN, I LOVE YOU
I LOVEY DVEYOUSUSAN I LOVEYOUSUSAN I LOVEYOU
SUSAN, U SUSAN, (FIND THE HIDDEN MESSAGE)OU
I LOVEYO LOVEYOUSUSAN I LOVEYOUSUSAN I LOVEYOU
SUSAN, I L N I LOVE YOU SUSAN, I LOVE YOU SUSAN, I LOVE YOU
I LOVEYOUS AN I LOVEYOUSUSAN I LOVEYOUSUSAN I LOVEYOU
Susan, I love you, Susan, I love you, Susan, I love you, SUSAN
I LOVEYOU SUSAN I LOVEYOU SUSAN I LOVEYOU SUSAN I LOVEYOU SUSAN
SUSAN, I LOVE YOU SUSAN, I LOVE YOU SUSAN, I LOVE YOU
I LOVEYOUSUSAN I LOVEYOUSUSAN I LOVEYOUSUSAN I LOVEYOU
Susan, I love you, Susan, I love you, Susan, I love you, SUSAN
I LOVEYOU SUSAN I LOVEYOU SUSAN I LOVEYOU SUSAN I LOVEYOU SUSAN
SUSAN, I LOVE YO AN, YOU SUSAN, I LOVE YOU
I LOVEYOUSUSAN US DVEYOUSUSAN I LOVEYOU
Susan, I love you you usan, I love you, SUSAN
I LOVEYOU SUSAN I DU SUSAN I LOVEYOU SUSAN
SUSAN, I LOVE YOU YOU SUSAN, I LOVE YOU
I LOVEYOUSUSAN I E YOU USAN I LOVEYOU
SUSAN, I LOVE YOU E YOU SUSAN, I LOVE YOU
I LOVEYOUSUSAN I LOV N I LOVEYOUSUSAN I LOVEYOU
, I LOVE YOU SUSAN, I OU SUSAN, I LOVE YOU SUSAN
I LOVEYOUSUSAN I LOVEY SAN I LO(Who loves you Baby)
SUSAN, I LOVE YOU SUSA LOVE YOU SUSAN, I LOVE YOU
I LOVEYOUSUSAN I LOVEYOUSUSAN I LOVEYOUSUSAN I LOVEYOU
SUSAN, I LOVE YOU SUSAN, I LOVE YOU SUSAN, I LOVE YOU
I LOVEYOUSUSAN I LOVEYOUSUSAN I LOVEYOUSUSAN I LOVEYOU
SUSAN, I LOVE YOU SUSAN, I LOVE YOU SUSAN, I LOVE YOU
I LOVEYOUSUSAN I LOVEYOUSUSAN I LOVEYOUSUSAN I LOVEYOU

THE TABLE

On the table long slim scissors,
a wristwatch, a book of
matches, thin wire rim glasses
Front page news no more menacing
than the yellowing tablecloth
Stacks of post cards from Europe
Dark marks left by a careless smoker
Long scratches made by a screwdriver,
deeper ones by a knife
You can trace the journey, feel the regrets,
almost smell the Autumn leaves burning
A high school teacher who
tinkered with electric gadgets
Back in the woods the tree house still
stands and the water is safe to drink
I still hear the shots fired at you
by that wonderful drunken tenant
Why didn't you trust me?
What was in your heart
that I couldn't see
You died alone---
You died
you

IT HAPPENS

It happens, every 27 million years or so---
I visit a hard rock cafe or get a new pair of glasses
Mail a submission to the Southern California Anthology
        A note will arrive a year and a day later
Sorry...but we only publish poets who
actually reside in California
It happens every week, I'll get a rejection slip,
a note in response to my question
Where is the diversity?
This editor says; I guess it's out there   Most of the
academic journals are formulated, banal and
pretentious Maybe you're not looking hard enough?
        It happened unexpectedly
A letter came declaring me free of debt plus a
new Cadillac with one coupon for a free car wash
The phone started ringing off the hook with
offers from universities to have me lecture
I'm holding out for a Bart Simpson doll
so I can tie it to the front bumper of my car
Cross my heart If I don't look those students
straight in the eye and say---
If you want success then stop writing and
open a clothing store in the naked city

In a secret place, half-buried in our hearts is the last sunset

MARCH 25, 1911

From the smoked-filled eighth floor of the Triangle Shirt-
waist Company they jump   From windows young women
cascade,spiral downard   Dear God!   the pavement so inviting

> Tonight---the breeze is a patchwork of misery
> Slave ships lost in the harbor or our soul
> Is there not a star blessed with our sorrows?

A human chain broken, the streets of lower Manhattan filled
with lifeless bodies   Brides-to-be, hair on fire, through the
quiet woods they streak, unaware of eternity, they fashion
a eulogy for autumn   A tenderness only a few of us will inherit

> The world unwilling to watch us die
> We are allowed only a moment to be a cloud
> Trying to be human, we whisper, *my beloved-*
> then shatter like glass   Not a day of rain follows
> to adore our beauty

The doors locked, horse blankets splitting in to two,
they jumped for the ladders, all of them missed

> In our loneliness we discover a poem,
> the language of loss, the random tear
> that reveals to us our own true face

49

LOST IN THE WOODS WITH EMILY

If I could walk on water - I could save the world
I didn't say I would   If I could walk on water
I'd charge admission for the first hour
What if I put four wheels on a postage stamp
and called it a Volkswagon
I'd bring Emily Dickinson back to life
         We would get lost in the woods
Her poetic mind tugging at the shoe strings
of inspiration while I struggle to
gather all the fallen leaves
I'd peek over her shoulder to see what she
was writing but wouldn't ask any questions
I would peel her an apple
and cut it into little cubes
         On cue she would tell me
Be grateful for what you have
         I'd ask her to laugh
Night after night I'd be a flat stone,
a small gray cloud that no one would notice
I would listen for the voices of lost children
Somewhere close are the bones of poetry...
But for now I close my eyes and think,
what a wonderful world if when we woke up,
someone would offer us a slice of warm bread

IN MY HEART OF HEARTS

They can torture me
Open my briefcase full of yesterdays
But all they'll find is an autographed
picture of Bob Dylan
A ticket stub, front row to
something called Woodstock
In all those years, all those miles,
if there is an absolute truth
I have not found it
Yet, in my heart of hearts I have
contempt for the unknown
Although, I believe my friend who
says that the Vatican has a time machine
in the basement
A letter is on its way to my lover to say
I have no use for the guillotine or history
I've discovered my wings and I am in
the company of clouds, Orpheus descending
Willing to sell my soul for all the trapping
of love in a dark theatre over both
fortune and fame
If death triumphs over everything at
least I have a fierce sense of pride
Knowing I never gave away a
good ending to a story
        Never---

A LETTER TO GLORIA

Gloria!
I am Andy Kaufman, Cool Hand Luke,
crazy...a poet
There is a poem inside my head
A shiny Doubloon and a rest room
token in my pocket
I am a concerto in G minor
My orbit in near approximation to the moon
        I am in love
        I am running out of oxygen
Yesterday, on Interstate 10 (the road just traveled)
Brush fires caused a twenty-two car pile up
Three people died
People are dying every day
A ten year old girl was
abducted in Gainesville
        What does it all mean?
Gloria
Last night I slept in my car under the
branches of a living oak in the parking lot
of the Country Baptist Church
I have lost your phone number
I am wearing Green Lantern's magic ring
I cannot find your phone number

In the rest room stall I heard Cuban refugees
praising Jesus while they mopped the floor
At the bus shelter a homeless person told me
he believed in Buddha---
I gave him my sunglasses
Gloria
What does it all mean?
Night before last I performed for nine dollars
What can any of us do with nine dollars?
I tell you the white sand is cold,
that Selena has found Puff the Magic Dragon
I told her on the street of dreams that we walk
they still hang the poor, the innocent
Mr. Tambourine man play me a song
        play for me 'til my heart
pushes on to Memphis
Gloria
How can I not but love you
Write my name in lipstick on every mirror
Gloria
Send me a tear—
Oh, this world that treats us like fools
        Sweet, sweet girl send me a tear
You are already mine

Not in the sense of flesh to flesh
but that already we conspire to share
each other's sorrow
The Beach Boys have left you a backstage pass
The Tokens serenading you with
   The Lion Sleeps Tonight
Someone asks where is Lakewood, Ohio?
Why is that important
I am not a slave to nor the master of poetry
I want the poem to name itself
I am a stagehand pounding nail
after nail so the poem cannot escape
Again I ask, Gloria...send me a tear
We are two large suns without planets
I am Shogun's companion
A swordsman at your side
I say Gumbo, you say Slingo
I say Jambalaya, mojo, two step
boogie woogie, Buckwheat Zydeco
and you laugh and laugh
It is October 1st, 1999
It is yesterday, it is tomorrow
Bush Stadium, the fifth inning
You are wearing a long white dress
Mark McGwire hits a ball deep
into centerfield

The lid on your music box is open
The baseball coming right at me
You are standing, rising out
of the ashes of all my failures
Rising out of Dante's wretched inferno
You are the actress you aspired to be
Why doesn't the crowd see you
The music is still playing
Santana blowing out the last candle
What happened to the baseball?
The scoreboard flashes a message—
  Gloria, will you marry me?
This moment to be shown over and
over as a black & white newsreel
My glasses knocked off,
everyone fighting for the baseball
I tell you it is madness
The hell with living
Give me something to die for
For the last time,
what does this all mean?

It is march 7th, Orlando
It is yesterday
It is tomorrow
It is the Earth beginning
All of it is as we wish
Gloria!
This poem is my tear for you

ON THE ROAD HOME

Whitman's wild children, the insanity of grammar,
the heartbeat of poetry trapped in a far off frontier
I for one am not ready to surrender
my life to the ambiquity of words
Mercy, courage and acts of kindness were
once the centerpiece of human existence
I tell this story for no other reason but
to totally erase my memories of it
Is it true that only boys can be mean?
After school I walked down to the playground
past serveral cats still hanging from a tree
The youth in question smoking a Lucky Strike,
grinning, proud of his deed
His soul nothing more than a painted prop
I wanted to tear his heart out
To this day I pray for a miraculous birth
Thank the prophet Elijah for the paper butterflys
I make out of the pages of proverbs
On the road home, Stop!

At work they asked, why didn't I back
up the car and put the thing out of its' misery
A black cat, half flattened by a car's tire
stuck to the road like fresh white lines
Front paws moving to reach the curb, unable
to drag itself from the rhetoric of doom
I kept going, a fugitive with a troubled heart
Running through the streets of Pamplona,
past the silence of the graveyards
Half the world and I being pushed
into a rugged corner
Somewhere out there the dog star was
trying to find me, to give me some comfort
I stopped, offered my heart a well-told lie
Standing off to the side of the road I was a
witness to the chaos, in awe of the beauty,
starring at the strange face of twilight

MARDI GRAS 97 - THE STRUGGLE

It's a cold Saturday morning and I'm tired from
playing the nickel slots all night in Gulfport
Tired from the long ride down here to New Orleans
After assembling my poetry wall on Jackson Square
some snob from the art league graciously informs me
to get the hell out here, to go across the street
After my wall is up again the police tell me to take
it down   Tell me I can't read my poetry
Hell! this is Mardi Gras You can show off your tits
Drink Jack Daniels right out of the bottle
You can moon the tourists, scream out obscenities
Excuse me, if I read some poetry I'll be arrested
I can't stand Jambalaya, crawfish pie or any
other of these Cajun delights
I am blue in the face
I am in the cafe Du Monde trying to get to a urinal
I feel like calling it quits
Because the eye is fooled by wooden fruit
Because we are a bologna sandwich
handcuffed to a park bench
Because junk mail clutters our living room
Because we are invisible
poets will always be ignored

BOSTON

(for Elizabeth Borges)

Before you left to go back to Boston
a beggar with one arm and the sad eyes
of David Bowie stopped us
As if he knew the future, so sure of himself
that he gave you all the coins out of his cup
Repeated these words twice;
   Great fortune will be yours, but not love
I helped you climb up a stone wall
Without hesitation you yelled out
   I'm young, cute, so take me - I'm all yours
You took half a step and fell into my arms
We heard sounds of tap dancing
on wooden steps We laughed, t
he hours unfolded like a lost
episode of *I love Lucy,* the whole day
slaughtered by a faithless world
You—-
so willing to settle for any empty promise
I didn't have the heart to tell you I was married
I remember touching a face without wrinkles
I'm getting old and the wind (or is it you)
keeps playing tricks on me
There are buttons missing on all my shirts
   Is Boston really that far away
     that I'll never get there?

IMAGES

A woman can be totally nude
and not show any part of herself
A woman can be laying down, bed
sheet arranged so the richness of her
form has you jumping through hoops
A woman can be totally nude and say
she is a glass of ice tea, the first and
last syllable of a haiku
Ever so subtle dissolve into our hearts
As you feel the weight of every
stone of the Pyramids pressing down
on you, a nude woman can be
a bruise, a flutter of helplessness
that a man tries to hide
A woman can be sitting in English class,
her dreams shipwrecked and washed
ashore in over a dozen novels
Yet, she still manages to stumble into
her arsenal of goodness, smile and
calm a nervous world
We are thankful, motionless soldiers
waiting for Bastille Day
To a man feeling the fierce
waves of lust and very much
mad with desire

STEADFAST

Because nobody pays
attention to small details,
eyes closed, almost asleep,
the moon (smiley face and all)
lifts itself quietly over
the backyard fence
only to be attacked
by howling guard dogs,
Their sharp teeth like a quiet laughter,
a fairy tale of double-winged death.
We look out the window,
the moon where it should be,
history repeating itself
as we hold on to our stubborn
beliefs, the privilege
of being human.

STURGIS, SOUTH DAKOTA

It's 106 in the shade - the lay of the land vibrates
like staccato rhythms - the grass anything but green
Shoes, socks off, left leg dangles out the window
U2 singing, *With or Without You*
I'm daydreaming of the ultimate seduction,
a Harley Davidson In the old days 250 bikers would
meet up at Wall Drug, (what the locals call the geographical
center of nowhere) They'd drink the free ice water and
buy some post cards   Peter Fonda, Easy Rider himself,
would take the lead to cover the final 100 miles to Sturgis
I have one hand on the wheel, a smile on my face as I
wave out the window at the fifty ton steel T-Rex with
the twitching ruby heart
       and you give...and you give yourself away
Beneath me is the soft belly of the earth - littered with
limestone - countless little caves that dream of moonlight
What I call the campgrounds of history
It's summer 1970, the start - the endings of love
affairs and I've tasted neither
Arms, legs bandaged from the accident
My younger brother's motorcycle unrecognizable
Honorably discharged and all I can think of is being
reckless, look out my dirty windows, thankful
I have no interest in poetry.

At Denny's classic diner, Harley Davidson's,
hundreds of them are parked diagonally,
like battleship row, a portrait of nostalgia
The sun reflects off the chrome, blinding someone
who's driving a corvette, they crash into a pole
Our feeble hearts jump for glee
We've learned to hate the distrusting quiet
The dishes will have to wait
You rummage around for your leather pants
There's no need to be reasonable
you want to finish the process, turn
the world upside down
Maybe some biker will notice you now
They speak of customizing, the details of the
rigid motor mount, how to attach a one
piece stretched gas tank   Heck! you don't
even need a touch up   They can talk all they
want about a twin cam, what you got puts
what they're riding to shame
You are Mozart's overture - let them tremble
Out in the streets, from every direction,
in every lane, night or day---
There is this undeniable truth
        There is a Harley on our ass
We have no choice
    We've got to love it

GRANDMA SNYDER

On sundays we would climb up the steps, knock
'til grandma greeted us wearing her funky (you
really need to wash this) silk white Diana Ross wig
In the kitchen my wife would listen to the
near fatal gossip from grandma She'd whisper
a clutching the National Inquirer in her hand
about two old widows in Florida who were
gagged and tied, raped repeatedly
It was an epidemic, without exception
a black man who always did it
Grandma had so many locks on the door that
Houdini would have a hard time getting in
Even I was becoming paranoid
Imagining dozens of black men canvassing
the neighborhood, working eight hour shifts,
metal lunch boxes in hand, like stealth
fighters evading the police, greeting each
other with the day's tally---

*How's it going Sam, Oh yea! she put up
a good fight, did she? I've had a busy morning
myself Rope, You out? Yea! wait, I got some
extra in my trunk*

After losing eight or ten games of rummy
to grandpa we'd head back home
Laying in bed, I felt slightly vulnerable,
yet safe within earshot of the street lamp

BEAUTY AND INNOCENCE

At sixteen we own the world
Owe nothing to our parents
Our bodies dance to the boggie woggie
of our new found freedoms
Much too old for children's games, we tease,
advertise our perfection
As to say like nothing you've ever seen
Like a classic '67 Mustang out of control
on wet pavement and because innocence
is an unwanted gift, we lose our virginity
In a heartbeat we strip, on a dare jump
off a grain silo
Because there are no second chances we
compose a perfect world,
then bleed all over the canvas
What hope we have comes from those few
who are willing to cry in our presence
We whisper to each other to make
sure we all still hear the music
If only we could believe in a simple truth
We would toss our heart's into the sky
Watch as they explode like
some wonderful obscenity

THE CURVED TUSK OF HISTORY

Let me break it down so you can understand it
Contrary to popular belief, in the beginning there
was a microchip or Bose radio emitting very loud static
The unsteady hand creating verse and universe
The Rosetta Stone dusted off by the rites of passage
The atomic bomb, paved roads and the great blackout
just meaningless equations on a blackboard
An abundance of beauty cutting off oxygen to the brain
Enslaved by evolution we buried the truth
even deeper in the snow   In their hearts
Neanderthal Man worshipped Cindy Crawford
Martian rocks fell to earth, some landing
in the glaciers to become keepsakes
Frame after frame nothing changed   Rivers kept flowing
Flowers blossomed, inch by inch man was coming of age
Starting out with the simplest gestures, grunts, we
shaped a language, realized we all cast a shadow
Without anger in our hearts we would have
to wait thousands of years for a holy war
What we now have is an over abundance of flavored
coffee   Water lilies in our backyards, CD disks
blasting out Tibetan chants   A microphone stuck in
someone's face, the doomsday crowd appalled
when they hear a poet scream out the words
                    Laughter comes easy—
Oh, what word of words
stirs the cosmic soul

OCTOBER 1, 1999

Busch Stadium, Cardinals vs Cubs
A choir of children sing the national
anthem while older adults glance up at
the sky hoping to find a favorite line or
two from a Billy Collins poem
I look out from section 593 and see
a bare stage, too many people wearing
red jerseys with the number twenty-five

        Before the Pinta, Nina and Santa
        Maria set sail to claim this land,
        only the flight of a cannon ball could
        rival the majestic arc of a home run

There's one reason why the crowd is here
Why they keep showing the holy relics
Frame by frame, the scenic route,
the push-mover sound of;
        going, going…gone!

There is some measure of madness,
a temporary sky protecting us from the
evils of the world
The Key is in the ignition
Play Ball!

It's the bottom of the ninth inning,
two outs
Chicago ahead by one run
Mark McGwire steps into the batter's box
Anticipation—
I move through the tunnel down to the
box seats by first base for a closer look
Hey Birthday boy!
Yea, you big Palooka
Some of us have come a long way
So punch us out of this factory of dreams
Don't disappoint us---

      Cubs win!
      Cubs win!

I place a Sammy Sosa bobble head
in my back window
The back seat loaded with programs,
dirty socks and under shirts
Just before getting back into my car I
hurl a fistful of stars back into the heavens
Thankful on my return home,
that Sammy is my co-pilot

UNTIED SHOE

Fourth grade,
you're the only
student
without a pencil
wearing
one shoe
without a
shoestring
Two apple pancakes
in your lunch bag
The only
one with
a poem
in your
heart

AUGUST 22, 1999

I have fallen like a wind swept napkin to the
bottom of this gorge, a place called Squaw Rock
Doesn't feel right chiseling my loneliness
into stone   A poetry book rests on bits
of moss and fossil-speckled shale
The sun like loud music, a soft
Salamander on my shoulder
I need to take all my clothes off, if not today
then soon...why?
Ask me after I've done it
I try to ignore the dogs that splash by
The poem and the day taking their time as Skunk
Cabbage clouds plow through the colossal sky
Wildly cool waters ask why my shoes are still on
I feel like laundry that hangs on a clothesline
waiting to be snatched from obscurity
There is more than enough here to keep
me happy   The language of colors to memorize
When the darkness comes I won't
be able to find my way home
My heart is a hug fire now
so the shadows come a little closer
If there is a heaven the
trees here have not said a word
Maybe, when the flowers bloom
I'll hear a rumor or two

STOPPING
THE CONTINENTAL DRIFT

It was the ice age, not enough
volunteers around to take a census.
No way of knowing how many
people had indoor plumbing,
or even bothered to use it.
It was the ice age, the stone age,
fire was required reading,
fur garments the rage.
Some genius taught a wild
animal to chase its tail.
One day someone starting singing,
another soul ectched a painting
on a wall, this lead to the wheel.
Something was happening,
revolution of ideas,
it was the patch quilt of progress,
beggars in the market square,
swords and shields.
It was slaves building empires,
the mind caught in the web of poetry,
the distant stars.
Who knew that one day we
could destroy history itself.

WATER

Early Spring, snows melting
The rush of water over
cold rocks like the sound
of soothing laughter
Salmon in search of
the impossible contry
Water swimming the sides of mountains
Cutting through the heartland
as it always does,
beyond the fossil record
The artist adding whitecaps to the painting
A small child walking into
the surf reshapes our reasoning
Atop a Manhattan skyscraper
lovers embrace in the rain,
proof enough that the earth
is still a garden
Does it matter how deep the oceans?
Surely the continents will sink again
Only man asks, how long will it take?
Adding my own tears to the
river of life after watching
Last of the Mohicans—
Love, not water, seeks
the path of least resistance

DEATH

The heat, the rain, the heat, the rain---
Heat...the HEAT is the madness
Hour by hour the cobblestones of
silence penetrate the soul
The red sun of our ancestors hidden
by the pale laughter of clouds
I'd count on my fingers to a thousand
　　...think nothing of it
I remember the smell of urine
Fear and helicopter blades baptizing the dawn
The rain eight months pregnant
Day in, day out, all of us bumping
into a nameless evil
　　　　Gentlemen, whatever we do,
　　　wherever we go, it never happened!
God! How did I survive the drugs?
I can't remember a word
In the middle of the night, nineteen year old
boys would wake up screaming, running wildly
from a nightmare into a worse nightmare---Face,
chest, arms and legs cut by the brush and thorns
At the U.S.O. on a makeshift screen we watched
and listened as Richard Nixon gave a speech
Perturbed, we all stood up and gave him
the finger, singing...
　　　　We want to get out of this place,
　　　　if it's the last thing we ever do
I'd give my last breath to
wash the canvas clean

ROBERT MITCHUM

I'm writing this because my wife never had a crush on you

    Standing in front of the mirror I repeat,
to the best of my ability I will not confuse
Robert Mitchum with Kirk Douglas, Dean
Martin, Burt Lancaster or Charlton Heston or...

Did any of those other actors write poetry in the men's
room or on gas station walls They would have loved to,
but it was you who tamed and pinned Marilyn Monroe
down to the ground in, River of No Return
   Is it true that Katharine Hepburn made
A comment to you---*They keep sending me these
good looking men instead of actors*
Maybe she needed to puff on some weed or ride the
rails with you, take one on the chin in a barroom brawl
She'd learn to keep her mouth shut, thank the stars for
riding shot-gun as you dodged the law on Thunder Road

For those of us who aspire to be tuff guys or cowboys,
you're our recruiting poster, a good luck charm called
nostalgia I say ramble on 40's and 50's forever

The odds are on our side We are dreamers destined
to become beachcombers of the abyss
You were always suave, yet continued to mystify,
giving us nothing but a hard stare
On some unknown highway off to the side of the road
in plain view you've dumped a batch of bad scripts
I, on the other hand am stuck---in a ditch
called the here and now

LAST NIGHT OF DRINKING

Late summer 1969
Twenty-one and home on leave
Before shipping off to Vietnam I peel around
and crash the red lights on Public Square
My buddies take me out for a night of drinking
(I used to drink back then)
I don't remember any of this...
The story goes that I ran out of the bar
and jumped into some woman's convertible
The light turned green and that was
the last time they saw me
When I woke up the next day my mother
scolded me for being dropped off by
a cab at 6:30am in the morning
I found a note in my shirt pocket
Just the word, thanks---
and a phone number
I never called, never found out
who I lost my virginity to

THE KISS

At the Rusty Nail Steak House soup
of the day simmers on a pot belly stove
Flames dancing like the Aurora Borealis
We ship red wine, the best they
had to offer, the worst we had ever tasted
Walking out by the river, The night sky hums
like a harmonica of fireworks
Damn you woman!
You know it's true---
The only sunshine to peek Inside your
dark tunnel of love was my Harley Davidson
We can write poems forever,
recite the ex-lover's creed
til Hell freezes over
But nothing will recapture the
passion of that first kiss
       Did we f---on the couch?
Such an obnoxious word,
such a wonderful act
Each lacking sophistication
Your scent, your beauty dripping
not like some mere Hollywood legend
that men worship
Your eyes a crucifix of desire
You were Snow White stepping out of
the brittle pages of my dream
Told me not to say a word, shhh…
Placed my hand over your breasts

Our silence dusting off the sacred altar
The palm of my hand soothing,
nurturing your hard Chocolate Chip nipples
What chance did I have, you?
It was the gold rush...
Two quarters, heads or tails,
Red lips like the streets of insanity torturing me
A sign that read---
        Welcome to Spitzer Dodge
   Nothing making sense
God! I almost forgot that
I loved ice cream
So you grabbed me, buried your
tongue deep inside of me
Overwhelmed by passion,
the decades juxtapose
We lost ourselves in an ancient forest
I became a blind man, fingers searching for
any crevice
Your kiss a bandage that
didn't stop the bleeding
You're gone now...
to Arizona, somewhere in the
desert searching for that
elusive cactus called true love
But before you change the face
of poetry forever
Before you learn to spell your own madness---
Baby please come back!
You forgot your Ruby Slippers

COAL MINE

The coal mine is a sunken ship
The foreman a wild man,
sits on a rocking horse and does nothing
but talk of his girlfriend in Milwaukee
The shaft is a burnt river, everyone chained
to the oars of a roman war ship
You see the outline of the ageless Sphinx,
smell the perfume of Nubian Queens
Your once pretty face but a reflection
of a starless night
Your two dollar smile scares the young ones
What's a fair wage for lungs that
will ripen into metal lunch boxes?
A century of progress
stays hidden in the wood pile
The rain false indigo
At school kids are taught
that Elvis is just a 29 cent stamp
Whatever is important to us disappears
into the wilderness of the eleventh hour
This poem ignores the days without end
The sacred harmony of Blue Grass
Spare change which
is the story of our life

DALI

The poem, the painting doesn't have to make sense
Some people insist everything has to make sense
Those are the people who lack imagination,
gargle with Listerine, fold their socks neatly
Hello Dolly, welcome to our world of visual
language, the joys of being controversial
I don't rely on revelations, just waking up in the morning,
just rich enough to afford a small studio,
it's called a number two pencil

The girl With The Curls - 1926

Looking at this painting I realize I'm frightened,
overwhelmed by the nakedness of my own desires
Dali is a master, the world a mouth he kisses with delight
Life is perversion   Art is perversion
We strive to twist, rearrange some truth - some artifact,
the process pushing evolution ever closer to its' final goal

The Phantom Wagon - 1933

Simple, blessed by the spectacle of beauty and the
crooked wheels of poverty   One of my favorites

*Gala Nude From Behind Looking In
An Invisible Mirror - 1960*

The image, a haunting likeness of my mother
I can touch her hair, feel the texture, the longing
Wishing she would turn around so I could know for sure

God bless the queen - our doubts
Deep in the heart there is a theatre full of empty seats
The weathered bones of Shakespeare weeping
like the Autumn wind
We are hostage to the flesh, of some comet
yet to be named   Overwhelmed by the stars,
the vast oceans of darkness,
the mystery of it all

SCHOOL

When they escorted
God out of the
classroom
they gave the devil
a sweetheart of a deal
Now he's turning up the heat
Our children petting him
like an old sheep dog
The small voice of the
soul silenced
Even the poetry they read
oozes from dark corners
    This blackbird,
paradise lost, the light
of day nothing more
than a raven—
    death

PAGE OF HAIKU

Where the rainbow ends
In palm of great Zen master
Morning poem for you

Good luck smiles on us
We ask for more of the same
Our dreams...paper-weights

When wars are over
Left behind in deep rubble
The book of small souls

There's so much beauty
It's a shame to rush through it
Close your eyes---kiss me

The fox in the field
The grapes on the ground spoiling
The last leaf falling

Overwhelmed by life
Half way across an old bridge
Sometimes one must stop

Here...this gift for you
An empty gasoline can
Please...go fill it up

IT ALMOST HAPPENS

All we want is to see into the future, for
a lover to scrub our back softly with a pumice stone
The present, too much of a conspiracy to unravel
So we read nothing but romance novels
    Waiting in the checkout line a stranger asks
Who are you, what are you searching for?
    It must be the sailor moon I think,
trying to seperate me from the familiar
I answer, I am a poet in search of a fabulous
island where everyone is extremely tolerant,
some outpost that repels horrible dreams
    I wait, then leave with my bags
Outside, a panhandler is holding up his sign
    it reads,
I am trying to escape the tedium of my existence
He's not trustworthy, his posture all wrong,
there is this air of affluence around him
    I just want to be left alone
To find someone who's willing to become
somewhat wicked - someone who will
make me forget about the *No Name Saloon*
There are some of us who are truely lost
Lone figures watching the sunset
Every goodnight kiss just a shadow dance
Fast asleep, the muse grants us a small favor
We're allowed to laugh, to share a tea cake
The dream half remembered
Storms on the outskirts of town
decide to enter other souls

HONEY MOON

for Bonnie

The lands...are all most beautiful
The people all go naked, mean and women...
They are artless and generous with what
they have, to such a degree as no one
would believe but he who had seen it..
Christopher Columbus

I am looking at a penciled sketch
of a naked woman holding two parasols,
surround by seagulls
Floating down to earth as though
whe was the last leaf falling
     Stop—do any of us need a reason to cry?
Niagra Falls, walking back to the hotel in a
downpour we laugh, chilled to the bone but happy
     We take our clothes off
Joyful hands explore the expanse of your breasts
Each day we ask for more of the same
Profit from the pleasure
     Years later,
the soul is starving for a kiss
     The heart knows nothing
If someone were to kiss me now
     the rain would never stop
The last leaf falling, falling,
        falling, falling—

LIT CIGARETTE IN THE NIGHT

I am the legendary tourist, star gazing,
strung out on the Moody Blues
A refugee from affluence traveling up and down
the highways, just a lit cigarette in the night
Somewhat of a madman who thinks
every woman is a poetry goddess
I stand on the hood of my car, swear that
South Dakota has vanished, gone are
the Black Hills, the roar of Harley Davidson's
Ameria, you're an obstacle course
and I don't have the time to navigate
through all these narrow straits of truth
Sing Judy Garland, point me towards the rainbow
Through my plastic telescope I see a swirl of dust,
for the love of the game, Jackie Robinson
is sliding into second base - again and again
Deep in the soul of America, this skunk-infested,
vine chocked, void-of-poetry troubled nation
I remain a Jack Keourac wannabe
I say, it's all nothing but loop-de-loop, a three
card Monte game to see who gets into heaven
            You can't pick up any stone
              You can't disturb anthing
                Can't take even one pretty rock
                Cause...they'll put you in jail
              Stick their tongues out like the Road Runner
Off the road - I see all this wealth of detail
Here, the best place on earth, all alone
I can be a word smith daredevil, a summer storm
Soon, just another place that will disappear

VETERANS DAY READING

An American flag drapes a large window
The room filled with a stolen silence,
the coffee free
The audience clutches love poems
that bleed from paper kisses
I am the sun but they worship Captain Janeway
A pity, they will never be old enough to believe,
    The truth is out there
I'm not the one to tell them
that the best hugs come from strangers
They want me to read or say whatever I want
Don't they know I'm the boy that cried wolf
A psychopath that stalks the English language
A voice unable to explain my own madness
I see the twin towers collapsing
There is no place to run - I cannot get up
The door is locked,
who cares if the wall are painted blue
I'm waiting for the angels to come back from
the killing fields with fresh strawberries for me
There are land mines everywhere
Nude paintings of women on the wall
I can still hear Pink Floyd, the music coming
out of a tiger's cage, some September's rage
    Hey teacher, leave the kids alone

There is this painting, an ordinary woman
Off color jeans pulled down by a savage
love that reveals an Alaskan summer
Her nakedness flashing on and off
It is only a painting
I am in the moment, in a country
called *home of the brave*
Cigarette in hand she defies every
onlooker, takes pleasure in my discomfort
Her breasts sagging from their own beauty
I want her to be a mail order bride
For us to escape this earthly forest
I glance at my reflection in the window
We are laying side by side
She is star dust, a bright dress
in a store window, a Hebrew proverb
pouring through a vaulted glass ceiling
The wall is still blue, the towers gone
My lungs filled with her smoke,
Marvin Gaye singing, singing to keep
all our hopes alive
After all, she might be someone
I could meet tomorrow
Shoes tucked inside her hand bag
A smile telling me it's no accident
that her blouse is halfway unbuttoned

HISTORY CLASS

We can learn a lot of lessons from history
If only someone would teach us
Decades ago I was attending college, the
professor showing his vacation slides of Eygpt
A dozen or so of his daughter on a camel
Both of them standing by the Pyramids
Shots of the sunset, the sunrise,
a close-up of his daughter smiling, she was
wearing glasses, had a crooked nose
At forty still daddy's little girl, nothing more
than an Autumn leaf pressed inside a book
This was World History 101
He told us how lucky he was to have
seen most of te ancient wonders
His journeys fresh in his mind, as though he
was giving orders to a long line of basket-boys
Digging numerous pits, happy to oblige for
a picture or two in his jodhpurs and puttees
We sat in class, our books closed, every ten
seconds we heard the click, a new photo to ignore
Every five minutes he mentioned that his
beautiful daughter was still single
Surely he thought it was some sort of curse
It was tempting, for the hell of it—
to call her up and ask for a date
How ironic if she wore wild jasmine
A modern day Eros taunting the gods
with their own secrets

TRESPASSING

Chances are—
men that desire everything in a woman,
who demand perfection,
probably have very little to offer themselves
These are the men who have never
watered a house plant
Who threw their text books
into the homecoming bonfires
Go ahead! point your finger at them
Tell them you are Cleopatra
That your miniskirt means, no trespasing
Spin them sideways 'til they
see the handwriting on the wall
But wait...someday you might run out of gas
or want to share a cup of coffee with a man
There are men worth cheering up
Because somewhere within the whirlpool
of our desires we seek to fabricate,
nuture the swelling of hope
A phone number is half-dancing in our head
For the moment there is the urgency
that one of us finds a match
to light this dark cave

STAGECOACH

It happens to most of us, in the middle of a long
afternoon of watching the classic movie channel
we doze off and miss the last five minutes
Freezing rain pelts the windows
We imagine we are in an old barn
What we remember is the 7th Calvary
parting ways with the stagecoach, a woman
waves her white handkerchief out the window
A cast of characters to hate and fall in love with
Smoke signals on the horizon, all the ingredients
to make us fearful of tomorrow
Alone, tired of cheating while playing solitaire
I wonder if there is any apple pie left downstairs
Out of nowhere an arrow underlines the silent beauty
of death, stuck in the body like an unfinished joke
We think, kill those savages
We have no pity, the days and hours so ordinary
How many times will we shackle Geronimo,
how many desolated places will we tell
him to call home? We continue to gorge
on the lies of history, to probe, harvest
the handmade treasures of the Southwest
Morning comes to America like a dry whisper,
dusk falls, we turn our headlights on,
up ahead a toll bridge, detour signs,
no vacancy sign flashing in Morse Code
We could take one last look back,
but it doesn't matter,
all our heroes are dead

REST AREA

After four nights of sleeping in the van,
broke, nobody interested in buying
my poetry books I stop at a rest area
It's Thanksgiving weekend
Free coffee and hot dogs
I tell the woman with the weary smile
that I'm a famous poet
She says she likes poetry
I give her a copy of my book and sign it
A nine year old boy hands me
a West Virginia map
Asks if I would autograph it
        I make a notation;
Hey kid, you better get straight A's
or I'll kick your ass
I wish it was true - the part
about me being a famous poet

Outside everyone is wearing their paint by the number
faces Chances are none of us will get buried by lava
or ash to become Archaeological discovers—

WOMAN

Woman...I kneel on my prayer rug, meditate-once
again try to trace you name back to a dark cave
Touching every erratic inch of your outline, this
poor man's Picasso   Woman...she is a scared flame,
pious - a rare beauty who insists on wearing
a derby on her head   Like every other man I follow
her tracks by a scent called desire
She is woman - a monolith - an eternal silhouette
that reaches out to comfort every child
I imagine her singing in the virgin woods, picking
only those herbs that would help cure the
madness of the moment
     She was never primitive,
before the spoken word wished for a handful
of books She understood the magic of her curves
Often would disappear into the tall grass
to avoid both man and beast
Surely it was a woman who first dared to fill her
lungs with the silent stars She likened herself
to the flowers - Crushed rock so she could hold
the colors of the rainbow in her hands, tossed
them into the sky to blind the gods to her desires
She had the good sense to put red on her lips
     Somewhere in the swirl of hopelessness - in
a village in Nigeria or Pakistan a woman will stop
in the middle of her many, many tasks - smile
     This is no small gift that she lays
          at the feet of the world

Mardi Gras
2000

HONEST EMOTIONS

Dare to be different
    Dare to be ridiculed
        Dare to be a poet

At the creative writing workshop I'm told—
    Quit trying to be a poet!
    your metaphor is too abstract
    For God's sake! show some
    honest emotion
My poem shredded to insure
a unifying theme, form—
all at the expense of my voice
Years later—the moon

has become a gift of no importance
From the limbo of lesser travails an old
shark's tooth washes up on shore
I draw a happy face in the sand
and let my heart walk barefoot
I imagine being in love again,
but the word become a familiar
obscenity

    Dare to be different
      Dare to be ridiculed
        Don't dare be a poet

The sound of a bell
This new century half-lost
our weary smiles

Wind in the branches
The grapes on the ground—spoiling
The fox in the field

When wars are over
Left behind in deep rubble
The book of small souls

Where the rainbow ends
In the palm of great Zen Master
Morning poem for you

Overwhelmed by life
Halfway across an old bridge
Sometimes one must stop

For a man who claims
to have done everything—why
Are you so helpless

LOCKERBIE COFFEEHOUSE

(for Brooke Blossom)

You are a lost soul, sun glare,
a Boston Kreme donut I have
tasted every single day of my life
All I can offer is poetry,
not the songs of a young man
Afraid to tell you I've been to that place
where your heart has vanished
These last two days I've
ignored philosophers in the woods
Searched the FM dial for *real country*
Damn it! You're everywhere—
Moving farther away on a crowded train
Someone please ask her, when has
the heart ever made sense of anything?
I will tell you a lie,
throw crumpled twenties into
a musician's guitar case,
take you in the back room
and give you a kiss
      But that would be too easy,
      too perfect
There will be no love letters!
No goodbys—
Just the bitter medicine of a short story
The endless road we all inherit
This shiny stone, an autumn
leaf you placed in my pocket

TOO MANY POETS

There are too many poets—
Not enough Elvis impersonators
and fun house mirrors
Too many poets who'd have better
luck if they sold life insurance
There are too many poets—
Not enough two-headed snakes
and Shirley Temple movies
Too many books on the
shelf that never get adopted
In crowded coffeehouses we scream
into the microphone to be heard
We whisper to be heard
Confessing a multitude of sins,
making up stories about our ex-lovers
We take off our clothes to be heard
So starved for attention, so compelling
our verse we even approach lynch mobs
Poets should stop expecting
applause and miracles on Tuesday
Perhaps when we stop
fooling our own hearts
Then, maybe people will start
listening to us

BUKOWSKI

Bukowski, you 'ol bastard, you
died when I was just starting to write
I would have loved to call you—
              ....even if you had hung up
I would have been grateful,
the umbilical cord cut
Charles, California was too far away,
so I chased your ghost in New Orleans
and walked away empty-handed
In a bar I winked at the devil
Stood outside small cafes and
book stores and read my slop
Nobody paid attention, the words on
your gravestone mocking me – *don't try*
You don't have to work at the Post Office
to be crazy or hate your job
Maybe someone needs to punch me in the face,
throw me out of my apartment into heavy traffic
So what if I don't drink, I'm no pretty boy either
Everybody wants to cash in
on a long shot – to be a poet
Guess what, don't confuse me with the losers!
If you can't enjoy life, what's the use?
I'm *betting on the muse* also, foolish or stupid
enough to think the applause is just for me

WAR...I KNOW SOMETHING OF IT

London....1941
The last vestiges of innocence
cling to a black and white world
It was the dark ages---the great ice age
Spitfires flying under the wonderful
canopy of chaos and hope
The British with nothing to
embrace but the mumbling darkness
Thank god for Winston Churchill!
The doughboys and the English Channel
Was this their last finest hour?

Back into the caves for safety,
thousands huddle in the subway tunnels
The walls of Jericho crashing down
Children screaming
Grown men crying in flimsy whispers
Mothers holding on to both
How many bombs fell?

Too many....far too many

Gay Pare', the benedicition of moonlight
Wars!   they diminish our chance of placing
a human image among the visible stars
War! I know something of it
But they studied it in earnest
It was a stroke of genius---
they didn't need textbooks
It was happening all around them,
a never-ending field trip

My parents met during the war---maybe yours
Hiding behind trees as allied fighters
splattered the canvas with unholy flesh

Today, we breathe without purpose
So busy looking for parking spaces,
we seldom have time
to think about humanity
To reflect on our spiritual longing
At the dawn of a new century
Typing with just one finger---
What right do we have to bitch?

SHE DIED A KING'S DEATH

We live to die
       Living as best we can
Our earthly senses asking—will there
be Chinese carry out in heaven?

Homesick, we conjure up images
of New York's Apple Annie
We stroll outside, pause to peek
around the next corner, nowhere
to find the outline of redemption
So compelling our need to be reborn
that the mind fakes its own death

A certain enchantment tickles
our sorrows
So certain of death that everyday
a yellow school bus stops
We look for someone to save,
to add beauty to our life's portrait,
but all we see are the faces of children
When we snap our fingertips they
turn into wild cherries
and bright purple lemons

Lately, I have been toying with the truth,
stripping it naked
So don't bring me small pieces of the sun
or clouds that have never cried
Don't tell me there isn't a parallel
universe, that there wasn't so much
`poetry written that the Earth didn't weep

One of many, I salute the end of
the twentieth century
Sing out loud the last two lines
of *America – The Beautiful*
The room, the backyard,
the sidewalks, even the streets
silent like an empty dance floor

We embrace a certain guilt
Bake cookies for our neighbors
Lift our voices in church
On a rare occasion we leave
behind an atlas of the heart
Some memento that rests
in our casket
Some destination beckoning
that comforts the child in us
The wedding ring on
your hand

TREES

When the early settlers arrived
in this country, there was one
collective thought
  God! Look at all the trees here
With hardly a sweat and a whole lot
of body english they cleared the land,
catching a glimpse of our true destination
Wooden structures, no bigger than
honeymoon cabins formed the first
life-size Monopoly boards
Town squares multiplied
After the revolution, long after the
age of steel, brick, aluminum
a thousand shovels in twice
as many hands dug deep holes
The skyscrapers became much too
tall and the elevators too slow
Happy hour, a Kodak moment
that exposed how pathetic
our lives really were
But something was missing—
We needed trees to make
things seem perfect again
Wrought iron benches and pretty
legs to muzzle our haste

Once again we took delight
in stepping on fallen leaves
Any of us to get lost in our thoughts,
to lean and rest against
a curved wall of bark
This church door that never opens
Why would anyone want to be a tree?
Silly trees, they have an after life
Coming back as toothpicks,
eighteen cent yardsticks, chop-sticks
or pencils with, ouch!---lead splinters
To save the trees, we should all use
stubbornness as our walking sticks
And, if a rose is for remembrance,
let this poem be a tree
A breath of fresh air and a song
of gratitude for Julia Butterfly

ROCK 'n ROLL MUSEUM

Mekkah Sunshine on stage
Show some love, show her some love
The band ready to rip it out
Mic check 1, 2——check-check
They want to do it
Play loud, 'bust' our eardrums——

Pen in hand, inside this windowed pyramid
I write about forgotten Tuesdays
and angels without wings
Born of anguish and fear
I pass out free suicide notes
S-l-o-w-l-y back away from the twinkle
in the eyes of Alice Cooper
I want to bump into Janis, Jimmy—
to tell them I won't allow heroin
or cocaine to be my saviors

Senior citizens ride up the escalator wearing
funky rayband shades, hands over ears
Someone should tell them, that's not cool!
Call it street rhyme,
or shapeless soul of memory
Throw a brick thru a window, again
and again—till it sounds like revolution

Alan Freed knew there was chaos,
a Zeppelin heading our way
He knew, whatever it was—
we held it our lungs longer

You want Rock n Roll history—
Its here! hints of red-neck humor, reefer madness
The cold ashes of high school
lovers who set the world on fire
How about the Staple Singers
        They did it the hard way, side
stepping ignorance (or was it just plain hatred)
            From our tears came the inspiration
            From our laughter the words, their songs
            Written in the shorthand of life, gospel,
            music.....God's soda fountain

inhale...   exhale...   Go ahead,
        its only Rock n Roll
I want to be that crazy fool forever,
        writing lyrics or poetry
I love being here in this glass house,
        this jail house
Its-all-rock-n-roll-to-me-house
Barely hanging on to my religion

Come see Elvis, the Beatles,
Little Richard and Chuck Berry
        This is holy ground!
Come see the photo of Bodiddly
backstage cooking chicken
The people that knew how
To make it *hurt so good*
        Come in out of the *Purple Rain*
Moon walk past Michael Jackson
Be forever young, rebellious and
        lost in the *Purple Haze*

SUNDAY

Woke up, knocked on wood
Somewhere on the concrete steps
the newspaper, a condom that
protects us from the truth
Kids are playing next to a
yellow house trying to catch
frogs with deformities to
count the extra legs
Where are you my ugly
faithful friends, have you
found a deep channel that's
hiding all the good news?
I spot several neighbors
peeking thru their windows
If three or four senior citizens
were standing around here now---
they would probably say,
   beautiful morning, isn't it,
we should thank God we're
alive to enjoy all this
I drive around, looking for a store
that sells coffee and donuts
At Shadyside I find a place
and sit down

Someone has stolen the welcome mat
The coffee tastes as bitter
as yesterday's MTV travel log
      What I really want is a new
Harley-Davidson
To have people touch the chrome
Out west is where I want to be
Before the countryside becomes
littered with music and plastic toys
Before all the cornfields
turn into *Field of Dreams*
Before Sitting Bull forgives the white man
On the Kansas plains I'll listen to
the windmills of poetry that create
goblins that sing like a choir of angels
Whatever highway I take, I'll leave
behind hundreds of wanted posters of me
Relentless in my love
for the *Goo Goo Dolls*
I'll sign the breasts of the
first waitress that lets me,
the words---
      I ain't scared of dying
If we make love
You best believe I won't
tell her, I was lying

NIGHT STARS

On the porch again,
looking straight ahead
An old man of fifty-one now
People say that's not old,
seventy-five, eighty-two that's old
I tell them I'm old enough
to say I'm old—and that's that!
Thirty-five years ago peeking through
this window behind my left shoulder
I saw some strange lights, they
were dialing in from an area code
outside our solar system
They reached in and rearranged my soul
I felt a connection,
wanted to be up there, to go with
them to their next destination
Seconds away from running outside——
they vanished, human eyes unable
to calculate their speed
Too young to understand any of it
Scared of this celestial note in a bottle
But they planted a seed in me and
every so often I converse
with the stars
I am somewhere out there,
in spirit and name

VENICE BEACH

Hot sun......Melon sky
Venice beach—
Take one step back and you'd
swear this was always a flat planet
The streets empty except for
the homeless who pray
for nickel lemonade
Flip a coin to decide if
you roller blade or pull
two hours of bikini watch
Some folks say you can find
everything you need here,
except a good book by a good man
Only here would you expect
the Dalai Lama to chant
> *Money is everything*
> *Only fools worship*
> *The blue green ocean*
On Sunset Strip the drunk yells—
> *I love a parade*

Black lipstick angels
(run-a-way Cajun queens)
blow kisses to poets unknown
So sure of the plastic crucifixes
they wear for protection
There is a blueprint for happiness,
but only bits and pieces torn
from the arms of Gods—
> ever wash up on shore

Last Call to Escape
Planet Earth

Last Call to Escape Planet Earth

To Escape Planet Earth

"The future's already here,
it's just unevenly distributed"

1.

As the last rocket ships
leave planet Earth I'm playing
the National Anthem
on my harmonica, waving
good-bye to everyone.

I'm singing this useless
song called *feeling sad,*
seventeen years of impersonating
a poet, living like a refugee,
banging on a makeshift drum
made from a run-a-way hubcap.
Powerless to save a cut off finger
or a leg or a child trapped
in the civil wars scattered
across the continents.
Where can any of us go?

One waits for night,
for an object to appear,
if only briefly,
a tap on the shoulder
as if to say,
    "catch us if you can."

2.

The stars are too far away,
it's 1956, I think my ears look
funny, history my best subject.
After school I'd rush to the South
Branch library on Scranton Road
to read from the pages of
"When World's Collide."

I grew up on the west side
of Cleveland, spent all my free
time on a mars colony,
had this horrible feeling
that Earth was not my home.

At the Garden movie house
on West 25th Street I was
the one voice screaming
for the creature to escape,
the one person who wanted
all the humans to be vaporized,
the only kid who could hold
his breath for over an hour.

At night I'd play around with
the radio, listen to the signal from
St. Louis fade in and out while
secret agents drove past the house
following something in the sky.

Wade Park VA Hospital

for Joann

I walk in,
find myself at the Atrium
standing in front
of the information counter,
get escort by a volunteer
to the urology clinic.

Questions—
did you bring your picture ID,
do you need help with transportation,
do people have a hard time
understanding you?
You sit quietly, no telling who
the enemy is, you didn't come
back from the ashes of war
to be fooled by a smile.

Seated in the waiting area
at the pharmacy I watch for my
name to flash on the tote board,
across from me a woman is wearing
a belt with dozens of keys—
all duplictes, she's jotting
down notes on where she
plans to loose each one.
I cry for her.

Many veterans are in wheelchairs,
oxygen tanks strapped
to the back like the Rocketeer.
The wives smile,
hold on to what's left
of the ghost's of greatness.

Jungle rot has kissed their faces,
a bloodied bandage all that's
left for us to call a nose.
We were god's on the battlefield,
so young the sun worshipped us,
a band of brothers,
we lived and died because
it was expected of us—
I cry for them.

Would you kiss a face like mine?

And what do I want...
I want you to believe in
small miracles,
that out of spare change
and matchbooks I can
build a mansion for you.
I want to be seventeen
again and be a Jim Morrison
look-a-like.

I want to know why it took
so long to find you, for once I want
to find something larger than
Noah's Ark in my cereal box,
I want the courage to stand
up in church and yell,
      Save me Jesus.

The windows on the Superior bus
are wet & dirty, it's gospel night
in the last three rows,
talk of the O'Jays
getting on at the next stop.
Three blocks from public square
an older man starts singing,
I hand him a fifty,
he's on his way back
to sing...
      "I'll be sweet on you."

From the mountain top
is not everything sacred
this beautiful Earth...

Sacred Links

By the campfire Black Fox tells me about
the spirit of the trees, how they guide us,
help in our spiritual journey.

The streets of Jackson Hole, Wyoming are
barricaded, federal agents along with forest
rangers guard the White House's
Christmas tree. The driver get out, tightens
the straps, an acorn falls off, rolls to the side
of the road within arms reach of you.

How is it that fire,
sky dissolve into laughter—
Vivid the images from
    March of the Wooden Soldiers...
At the AA meeting I confess that my past loves
are nothing but headless saints, that I worship
my cruel life, fearful of being healed.
I hand the pine cone to a stranger, my soul
cleansed by the noise of a passing Santa Fe train.
I want conversations to be like silent movies,
so I'm back on the road to nowhere, searching
no less than for the pharoah's daughter.

Wheat For Bread

Who will sing for me?

1.

Wheat for bread,
because 1948 is the year of the rat,
because black birds fall out of the sky
the world insists you invent laughter,
write poems for the lonely.
Because you have a gentle voice,
stranded on the island of lost children
America decides to bloody your nose
so you betray your ethnic heritage.
In winter it's cold, too cold to tip
your cap to the headless angel
atop St. Michael's church,
lake-effect snow forcing
you inside the Mars Restaurant
on West 25th Street to warm up,
order French Toast,
your first cup of coffee.

2.

We came to America to live
and stay in the great belly of the cities.
Some of us walk the horsepath down
to the Cuyahoga , under
the banjo & mandolin bridge to start
our fires, to drink what's left
of our most precious gut rot,
to forget our names, some
to forget where we came from.
Forgive me for living in the midwest,
for being honest enough to say
that Jackson Pollock was no artist,
that only now I'm beginning
to understand that art is the war
itself, the face in the mirror
a cracked blue vase in need
of two brush strokes.

3.

As a young man I would of chosen
to hang at the end of a rope
along side the sons of Scotland,
to march in step with the Devil's Brigade,
freeze to death in the trenches with
the sixth army at Stalingrad.

Today–
the VA doctors have prescribed
a generous assortment of pills,
told me to hate the person in the mirror.

I have thrown bread on the front lawn
for the birds, put the washed clothes
in the dryer, the rest of the day
spent wondering what kind of death
am I practicing for.
How lucky this skinny old man was
to snap a picture of a double rainbow,
in protest lay down on the grounds
of an atomic test site & felt
the rage of the world.

Hiding In Our Own Skins

for Anne Sexton

I met you in your poetry,
just once I wanted to ask you
if rowing towards God was like
riding a dead mule.
We R who we R,
nobody's perfect,
I'm addicted to lip balm,
every thought of mine remains
a secret, I find it impossible
to share my emotions.
Can you help?
Perfectly splendid,
I'll consider your silence a yes,
I will dress you in the likeness,
the dogma of swift clouds.
Your name, my good deeds will get
us into Shangri La.
Take my arm, we'll mingle,
it's ok if we don't understand
our unhappiness,
and no matter what they
tell us we'll keep dancing,
swallowing our green pills,
our skin on fire, burnt
offerings for the gods.

Homecoming Dance
—for Shirley Wilson

It's all about the music, slow dancing,
dragging a lame foot across
the dance floor in step with the fiddle
and Queen Ida's Cajun beat which
is enough to be called a hero.

You miss tag football,
walking someone you like home,
watching fist fights in the school
yard after the last class.
How you loved being the only
boy in typing class, exceeding
sixty-four words a minute.

In biology class you closed your eyes
like a girl, filtering into Room 204
the misgivings of free verse from
Patterson NJ while the blond next
to you taunted the teacher with her
slender and sofa spread legs.

At the homecoming dance I sat
in the bleachers, felt like an expired
coupon, went to the punch bowl twice.
After an Elvis song I put my hands
in my pockets and walked home slowly
past the barber shop with comics
in the window and an unopened
box of 1965 baseball cards.

It's All About Me

You are a gift to the world,
a triple bank shot of undeniable genuis,
the manly version of Miss Piggy
yelling, me, me, me...
and hell bent on becoming
a cinematic wonder.

I navigate life by leaning on the horn,
dancing with a gravel eyed mop
to embarrass Gene Kelly,
writing my life's story in capital
letters on a lopsided porch swing.

You must understand that the left
side of my brain is a distant cousin
who never writes, sneaks out for
joy rides, crashes into trees.

I was a child of much promise,
first on the block to get a polio shot,
met Jack Kirby and Stan Lee.
At sixteen I learned how to drive,
made sure the road ahead was clear,
put it in reverse and floored it.

Applying For A Grant

Only on this planet can one find a copy
machine at every post office.

It says four copies of everything,
must be stapled, must have cover letter,
postmarked before the end of the world.
Double spaced with one inch
margins and you better have had
orange juice with your breakfast.
Two additional copies required, one set
not stapled, if instructions are followed
your application will be discarded.
It is advised you send more copies
than asked for, there is no such thing
as too many copies—
Extra copies appreciated.

We are the Borg—
extra copies will only
delay your assimilation
you will comply,
resistance is futile.

Before your inner little Buddha
explodes, remember some things
cannot be explained, as in how
many copies are needed
to apply for this grant.

Already The Sky On Bent Knees

Love is imagined
Poetry is imagined

The weather channel informs us that
already the sky in on bent knees, the
promised sunshine nothing but a dwarf sun.

What is not imagined—

Bibles thrown out to litter empty parking lots,
dead perch playing pinochle on Lake Erie shores,
relatives who cure headaches by picking
poison mushrooms.

An eight year old girl watches out the
window, her eyes a lantern full of fireflies
she waves good-bye,
wanting someone to wave back.

We are born not knowing the real names
of our urges, taught to say please and thank you.
I've tried, wanting to tell her that innocence
is a faraway place. The ghosts of lover's past,
every woman who ever smiled at me fill the
streets of a mind overrun with rioters,
the day reduced to pacing on wooden floors
about the letters that never came.

In the service of my country
I have become the afternoon of misery,
forger of dreams, rooftop lover,
conspiracy of the month devotee.

What the poem is trying to say,
memory is a road sign, a forgotten to-do list,
a dusty road named Alynn, her brown hair
like a flag flying over an old fortress as
American industry an old airfield beckons
to our transplanted faith like a love goddess.

I throw this out to the quiet sky,
kisses are like a music box being open,
snow storms that remind us of the
sudden rage of woods and hills
that taught us a thing or two
about getting lost,
the sacred journey that begins
with you eating all your vegetables.

Fragments From A Long Life

1 Deep Well of Disapointment

There's just a few words, a few precious
seconds to arouse the interest of the reader.
How about I just cleaned up some raccoon
crap in the attic, found old photos of the ex-
when she was too beautiful to look at,
too beautiful to ravage. (all this is true)
Two ticket stubs to a game C.C. Sabathia
won before he went to New York,
the only place his ego could
become bigger than his huge self.

Here's an old moldy program book
from the comic book convention held
in downtown Cleveland in 1973,
I was the chairman.
Off the streets someone brought
in the first superman comic that a dealer
bought for a thousand dollars.
In the Lincoln room we had
non-stop movies, slide shows, writers,
artists, the money was pouring in.
I was at the Kon Tiki having cocktails,
signing autographs, being interviewed
by the Village Voice, filmed for
the nightly news, (caught up in the
corruption of my own stupidity)
living out my dream.

2 Krazy Komics

In the basement,
closets,
bedrooms
and floating in mid-air
from a lazy eye
were tens of thousands
of comic books to read while
waiting for the 12th planet
to be discovered.
I loved them,
modern masterpieces
to be traded with neighbors
and other collectors.
The wife wanted me to grow up,
to get rid of all of them.
(never listen to a woman who
doesn't believe in your dreams)
She wanted a man instead of a boy,
so one day I sold them all.

Gone the fragrance of history,
egotism,
secret identities,
my little empire wiped off the map
forever.

Here's what I should of done
cornered her against the wall,
with one hand undone the snap,
uncovered one breast,
looked her in the eye and said,
you love this more than you think.
Then waited, letting that
one breast face the dangers
of moist lips or worse,
to be ignored,
to orbit a planet like
a cold moon.
      I should of said,
   I believe this one is cream-filled,
   thinking to myself, that is so true.

I know my eyes would play a tug of war,
I would have to think as if a little
boy on an errand,
keeping myself preoccupied
with something trivial,
walking the isles looking
for potato chips,
to wonder what all that
noise was about coming
from my parent's bedroom.

3 I Stood There Once

To whom does the heart speak—
one shoe blues,
rolling paper in our pockets,
all of us wanting to hitch a ride
to San Francisco to become
part of the migrating prey.

We listened to the Grateful Dead,
Moby Grape, Santana, feeling the love,
doing something that pleased us.
Marching to the beat of rebellious hearts
we became part of a great movement.

I was there, my heart twisted into colorful
peace symbols. In the theatres on Market
or Castro Street or at the Bijou
chances were that a sailor would
put his hand on your knees.

Years later
it would all come full circle,
men's faces fading like
the poor soil of gentleness—
muted like the color of stone,
the nights coming alive
with candles and torch lit sorrow.

Today I walk the seven acres
of the AID's memorial in broken
silence, drowning in a river
that swallows all things.

4 Thin Halo Of Morning

I would wake up each day without saying,
Good Morning Jesus, I need to trust in you.
The 70's, Chevy's and Ford's were rusting
out faster than sex in a back alley, hubcaps
and bumpers littered the highways, Richard
Nixon our beloved Pinocchio, Vietnan,
nightly news from the siege at Wounded Knee.
(the only good citizen is the uninformed one)

I lost my job at the steel mill,
gave up listening to the Oak Ridge Boys
and gave my soul to MTV.

I disappeared into the vast underground
economy, living in the back seat,
hustling out of the trunk of my car.
Traveling from New Jersey to Florida
to Tennessee, (sleeping, waiting
in the car for hours before McDonald's
opened for a cup of coffee) selling photos
of Marilyn Monroe to day laborers who
couldn't speak a word of English
but paid with tired smiles three dollars
to place her on their altar of poverty.
I'd run into my friend from Calcutta
who had more than enough gold chains
on display to fear for his life.
In a steel cabinet in the basement the
money grew to a stack seven
and two third's inches high.

5 Legend - Legacy

On Campus I find a quarter on the ground,
remind myself to wash my hands.

Woody Hayes never faced
a team from Gillette Wyoming,
only cared about winning,
so faithful to the running game
he wouldn't allow a *Hail Mary* pass.

Ohio State University, Thompson Library,
the invisible hand in bold letters
leaves on the floor the rubble
of hope in verse,
the camouflaged history from clay tablets,
all that remains of Babylon.
Walking up glass steps who do I bargain
with as we dress in the ransom
of Chernobyl's victims,
of battered women,
the prospects of global peace
piled high with dead bodies
in Darfur, Bedi-Goazon, Rwanda
buried or waiting to be burned.

Those who were shooting said nothing.

Lord,
have mercy on us.

I have loved.

Ten Umbrellas

It is all Madness, random words,
small details shouting themselves hoarse
on the cover, the poet's name slowly
climbing a ladder to get a peek at the
next world.
In southern California I spoke
with a man who was blessed to have
touched a blue dolphin, who always
kept ten umbrellas in the back seat
for the homeless, who let me drive
up the mountain road to discover
how truly vulnerable we really are.
It was there I smoked my last cigarette
and walked back to the car wearing the one
shoe I didn't throw into the blue eyed lake.
Returning to Ohio I road my bicycle
in a cold heavy downpour, eyes shut in
elbow to elbow to broken knee traffic,
I felt liberated, waited for an outgrowth
of humility, the chaos of history nothing
more than pennies thrown into
a fountain to become burning books.

Impoverished

These were hectic days,
seagulls flying backwards,
the beloved Southern Theatre sold,
to become the Paris Art Show.
Nightly at the box office
men's faces fashionably hidden
by a folded newspaper.

Most of my friends were working
at a Ford or Chevy plant, going
to Pink Floyd concerts and getting high,
and what did I have but a dark trouser
army of soup cans cleverly hidden
side by side in a corner.

You walk out of the house with
just enough money for a cup of coffee,
stop to listen to the gossip
of old women, check the dumpster
in the parking lot for anything
with instructions on it to tell you
what comes next, the police about
to stop you and ask for some
form of identification.

Listening To The Heart

Tender are the young

Elementary girl kisses boy,
teacher calls administration office,
police are called in to determine
if a crime has been committed.

—kids,
come sit on my porch and misbehave,
I'll go inside to dust off the coffee table,
reset the doomsday clock then
straighten up some magazines.
While I debate my receding hairline
about the origins of the universe
you'll have enough time to reclaim
ownership of your innocence.

If they hunger for a kiss it's because they
have been faithful to a darkness filled
with flying monkeys and broken promises,
a future in peril, the ever shrinking
twilight of reality we create for them.

Let them kiss—
so happiness becomes the touch of summer,
so love knows where the hidden key is,
the ear so close to the heart we can hear
it purr, that a child's laughter is the first
and only clue in our search for true love.

The 'Old' Arcade

—I love the sound of their walk,
the hush of high heels,
        the square marble clock,
Roman numerals tickled by
a large minute hand that finishes
a circle waltz every hour.

The Hyatt lobby is no fake autograph.
Twelve hour days, immigrant pride molded
by stubbornness, tales of Moby Dick
and bruised egos of the twentieth century
are etched in glass, surrounded by the silkworm
simplicity of depression era art deco.

Ceiling fans spin like the blurred headlines
of the printing presses of the Hearst empire,
gossip revival, the undercurrent of political
cronyism and industrial might.

Five stories up 44 cast iron griffins proclaim
summer's end, a hour is a minute a minute
is an hour, poetry the ultimate seduction.
Seated at a round table I look for something
sacred wanting to wake up to a world
of Muddy Waters and Thin Lizzy.
The fingers belong not to the hand,
a teaspoonful of crazy love,
this moment—
like an unfinished canvas.

Somethin Stupid

Julia,
you are the guardian
of late antiquity,
adorned by the robe of kindness,
too many days having past like
a priest with no offerings
for the promised savior.
May the warm sun of dark coffee
and these words greet you.

Don't tell anyone but this is really
a conspiracy poem,
a note placed frantically under
random windshield wipers,
the brotherhood of erased history
about to shut
the door to our curiosities.

Have you read Plato,
felt the world unravelling,
nothing around to grab hold of...
The future is a blindspot,
please, a minute to explain forever—

> *and then I spoil it all*
> *by saying somethin*
> *stupid—*
> *like, I love you*

Miss Frances is ringing the bell
and I'm ready for Ding Dong School,
hands folded on my lap,
a small wonder that I haven't
left the house for years,
fearful that the Northeast wind
wants to steal my umbrella.

I'm busy on my Marilyn Monroe project,
washing my hands fifteen times a day
just like she washed her face
that many times.
      Wait—
I do not worship her,
women have spelled doom for me.
      Wait—
I am the curator of a thousand dark blue
warped and worthless *Space 1999*
bumper stickers, a basement door that's
completely covered with *Howard The Duck*
for president posters.
      Wait—
is that the glory bound bus
about to stop at my house?
      Wait—
off the road of one's two lane highway
of the mind is a wayside cross,
the heart demanding you pick up a pencil
and write about your unhappiness,
confession of sorts to be
whispered in Marilyn's ear.

Seated at the table with remarkable
women, the freshness of conversation,
talk of a frost warning for the next
day, running away from a secret society
of my own making,
an invitation—

Am I not lost in the Byzantine woods
that protect me, without a name
to answer to. In the distance a woman
lights her cigarette as if to say—
Its grown unfamiliar, a man's touch.
Not-so-far-off the secret spell of mushrooms,
the arguments overheard between
our parents, the stories we use
to hear as children that our
silly hearts believed.

Whose Goose Are We Cooking

The fox has broken
into the hen house,
it's quiet,
he's too late,
they're all on vacation
in the Bahamas.
The lucky ones
are being roasted
with great care & glee
on the finest beaches,
those with
slightly red eyes
mistaken for chickcharnies
meet a more awful fate.
The fox is still hungry,
the quickness of his walk
brings him to a clearing,
the fresh smell of fallen apples,
the wide open
door of reality.

A Thread of Humanity

I secure and lock my bicycle
and enter the art museum.
I'm in love and her name
is—*all the time in the world*
to do whatever I want.
I've watched artists paint then enjoyed
late meals with wine, told them I'm a man
of rags, that I love watercolors,
the flowers they bring in from the garden.

Oil on canvas, oil on wood, nothing
interests me—I play around with my
imaginary double loop mustache, much like
that which graced the face of Salvador Dali.

A pile of clothes on the ground,
        pardon the mess,
each object a homeless person,
        there's no need to hide our money,
a guessing game of sorts that's
too abstract for me,
        the horror show of pennies
        underfoot,
a yard sale of the half-wanted,
pockets inside out.
        I yell out,
hey man, the jeans need to be washed,
hung up to dry on a thin branch of metaphor.

I've walked in their shoes, meaning
I'm about to steal the size eight black ones.
These clothes are drunk with dirt,
the room overcast with dirty socks,
blacktop shirts to remain a house of strangers,
the dim light helping to escort us
back into the cafeteria of guilt.

I know people, friends,
who don't believe in helping strangers,
that won't go to funerals,
who never keep their promises.
Not far from the museum outside a cafe
a woman sits on the sidewalk
in need of help.
How many of us would walk
away from a newborn daughter?
    and what did I do...

9/11 Remembered

Brenda, John, James, Perry—
the Exxon rest room is filthy,
the newspapers nothing more than
bean bags, throw away rags,
lost combs on cracked pavement.
The world has its truth,
      atop the George Washington bridge
      a large American flag (old French &
      Harlem laundry) offers itself
      as an armrest for the wind.
      I hear bag pipes in Central Park,
      look in awe at 50,000 white ribbons
      of hope tied to the iron fence
      around St Peter's church,
      one heart,
      my heart —
      walks down Greenwich St.
      offering to trade my new shoes
      for an old Yankess cap
      or a kiss from a stranger.
I watch green rental trucks head out of town
on the expressway along the Hudson
with all the evidence, the proof to all our
conspiracies that we hold so dear.

      9/11
      I can tell you this—
      Curious George and the man
      with the big cowboy hat
      had nothing to do with it.

The "Do Not Disturb" sign is everywhere,
pizzas being delivered seven floors up,
off llth street and near pier 49
a young couple sits on a blanket
having a picnic, news of the outside
world reduced to one tree
and the shrubs around them.
I praise the joggers, wink at
the Statue of Liberty that's blowing
kisses to the crowds on the ferry.
At a table at One Fish, Two fish restaurant
a find a coupon from Bed Bath & Beyond,
this will become my road map to the future.
I feel stupid paying $12.00 for a pack
of cigarettes, no money
left for a Broadway show or a taxi,
walking, walking, walking,
writing a message on a white ribbon
that says "Remember to Love."
I am blessed to be lonely,
to have given my heart to a woman,
to have faced death and realize
that I'm a coward.
I'm a poet eating a jelly donut,
at the moment a moving target,
so don't ask me to stop,
I'm too busy telling the world that
the NY cops look good in drag
and people are laughing again.

St. Mark's Bookstore

Already today I spilled a cup of coffee
inside a souvenir shop, almost
got hit on 7th Avenue by a car.
New York will say, *excuse me*,
and push you aside,
(like the woman in the black
business suit who almost
knocked me to the ground)
it will not stop to give you directions
to the #6 train so you
can get off at Astor Pl—
It's late, two blocks from St. Marks
Bookstore some folks are
holding cardboard signs for help.
They are out of money,
clean socks & razors, out of options,
if we don't listen to them
we will listen to nobody, learn
nothing of importance about ourselves.
There must be something around
to rub that's like touching
Buddha's belly for luck, some
sign that our fortunes will change.
I hand over to one of the guys
my chapbooks and the book bag,
He says, *thanks, maybe*
I can get a dollar for these.

Penn Station

New York City women at Penn Station
I need to borrow your umbrellas,
those dark glasses you wear to hide
your sorrows & copper cream eyes.
I want your earings—
those blue suede boots you're wearing.
None of you is Annie Hall but don't despair
you are perfect replicas of my fantasy.
Pardon your mean looks,
those big breasts, the purple
sweater that's tired of saying, ouch!
but I want each one of you.

Gevo,
your real name is bombshell,
I feel obligated to warn you
that beauty is an unjust monster,
and I the poor fellow who carelessly runs
after his wind blown hat to fall to his
death at the bottom of the Grand Canyon.

You can't do New York on three dollars
a day and three hours sleep, but I have
on the backs of other poets, sucking dry
the wallets of those who consider
me a friend, lighting a candle and listening
for the whereabouts of the homeless.

Tourists are busy taking pictures
of the actual nuts and bolts
of the Brooklyn Bridge.
I'm standing still,
on its wooden sidewalk feeling
the vibrations of disappointment,
applause from the Ed Sullivan theatre
as the Beatles bring down the house,
the midnight recoil of the F train,
alone in my thoughts at the same
spot that Sonny Rollins and others
would come to practice,
to re-discover their artistic souls.

It gets old...
hours spent standing in line
to get into the Nuyorican,
listening to cast-offs from
the KGB bar, confessions of young poets
about their fucked up childhoods.

Not too far from Wall Street
Friends of the Earth have gathered,
occupy Wall Street is a chessboard,
the morning train of uncertainty
released back into the ice age, the rich
saving their white beachtown skins
from the real climate change,
doubling down before
the final NY Post headline.

The universe has become
a frightened bird, the public library
that won't answer the phone,
two dollar muffins that require
serious smash and grab tactics.
34th Street station, two violins,
one mini cello, the sounds are
a flash of worlds, untold stories,
backyard tree climbing,
and to make myself feel better I cry
tears for myself and my father,
the hours spent watching my dad fixing,
bringing back to life gadgets
with tubes and wires
that were left for dead.

Lines Jotted Down On Soup Cans

Twelve things very woman
deserves now.
Best little black dresses
for under $79.
Instant sex-life reboot.
These and other catchy little blurbs
on the cover of magazines stir my
front porch rocking chair imagination.

But the reality is,
I'm still cold, not wanting anyone to notice
my graveyard muddy shoes from standing
by the noisy falls in Elyria, my grand-daughter
and I protected by large rocks and signs warning
us we shouldn't be here as trees and
large branches rush past as though around
the bend gasoline was just $1.09 a gallon.

I'm compelled to tell you that I like shirts
with one pocket, that Chicago is a big city,
you can hide an authographed
Ernie Banks baseball, but not for long
before somebody swipes it.
For weeks I've played over and over
"I want a man like Boozoo" ignoring Zydeco
classics like, "On a night like this" and
"Who stole my monkey."

The mind wanders,
   You're sitting on a piano in a vacant factory
   tryng to convince yourself that
   being poor is living a charmed life,
     the only noise is the well-dressed
     silence one hears after a knock
     on the door,
       so you start singing—

I'm special, so special...
so give me some of your attention.

The days are mixed up,
I am a little kid holding a balloon with
no idea where my comfort zone is.
Monday 9:00 pm, a new episode of
The Event on tv, is $34.00 enough
for a black dress.

Friday, outside Jacob's field wearing
an Indian's hard hat a temporary worker
carries a sign "When you need to call
a plumber, call us" he's holding a 60's
Japanese transistor radio, bent antenna,
proudly displays his minimum wage
Smile and is dancing around like crazy.
The you that I never knew...
should I tell you how you can have
gorgeous skin in just seven days?

Wednesday, at the International film festival
I scream out, "Hiding in Cleveland hasn't
Worked out, the news keeps finding me,
bombings in Libya, unrest everywhere,
to much of killing of the innocent". Escorted
out I miss out on "Polkatown USA" but still
manage to steal some chocolates to give
to you at the workshop.

In this beautiful city how many
of us lost in our own social experiment,
a boring life filmed in poetic subtitles,
this three page poem folded neatly,
placed in an envelope and handed to you.
        The last line to remain
          a private conversation.

Am I crazy or are you irresistible,
go ahead ask me how excited I'd be
to have a cup of coffee with you.

Endless City of the Mind

—the *Enterprise* is suddenly hurled
    millions of light-years thru space.

New York City tour bus leaves in five minutes
for lower Manhattan, a few drops of rain easily
wiped off on the top deck, for some this is
a pilgrimage, the heart ready to trade tomorrow
in for yesterday, our senses confused
by the graffiti of time.

Open a map of Pennsylvania, follow
a trail called I-80 to exit 161, head south
to a place called State College, enter
the university library, pretend this
is the welcome center for the entire
human race, your favorite soup along
with three slices of wheat bread awaits.

Memory is a closed road, walk the streets
of honeycomb nights, toss cards and toast
into the air because this is Fifth Avenue,
you are alive, part of the Rocky Horror Picture
Show, once again the world not making
much sense. Wait for the light to change,
then walk, walk...

Because The Moment Is Gone

"The world is too much with us:
late and soon".

Hemingway is off somewhere on his last safari and

I am a playful little black cat keeping an eye on my

neighbor who believes every woman is a fallen angel.

Those wind chimes of his acting nervous, or is it me.

I have created my own dark room, a small cage that

shapes one man's penniless odyssey, who collects rain

water from the jumbled nerves of the broken gutters,

There is a lawn chair, endless hours spent

in the sun, a sign I've been meaning to put

on the front yard to explain my madness.

Skeeter Davis, the cartoon network, Charlie Pride

the only stitches that heal a lonely heart.

I am marching into the fires of global peace,

I am Thor's hammer, mangled fingers gripping

a pencil as a small act of defiance,

an old man who surrenders to no one.

At the risk of admitting I'm human the world

steps in, once again knocks gently on your

door and asks for one last kiss.

Too many of us meander around burden

with a love we never get over, those

memories to remain as sacred ground.

I have become blue sky and ash, honking the horn

and waving at third graders, a hostage in the path

of two dismal futures colliding, one of the ugly faces

of truth, a short-tempered Vietnam veteran who has

marched to hell and back. Sitting on the front porch

I want the church doors wide open so I can hear

the joyous shouts of Hallelujah—

The gossip of the universe rushes to our ears

as silence, no more to it then that.

- Jawbone Open -

for Maj Ragain

The beats tried their best to open
the flood gates of poetry, like migratory
birds they plopped down on the west coast,
not unlike Burning Man they became
participants, relished the colorful thrill
of words and dared to *Howl.*
We were still babies, school kids raising
our hands to be excused, running around
the hazy back country of Cleveland, Kent Ohio
nothing but a few cold tears on a map.

The race to the moon over, we couldn't
find the golf ball, no reason to come back.
The view of planet earth priceless...
and that was the rub.
Maj Ragain teaching the young how to
write poetry before they could hold crayons,
instructing grown men and women to write
down the names of small fishes,
poems about peace. Once in awhile
someone took aim at a glass house,
and the noise got our attention.

Maj I still have your old letters, words
of encouragement, directions for getting
to John Brown's tannery at the river's bend,
the recycled joy of homemade pies baked
by Jeff Ingram for the Jawbone that
helped us walk through the needles eye.

A thousand magazines born, put to rest,
the small voices of aspiring poets,
latch-key children holding tight their
dog-eared chapbooks needed a place to read.
The Jawbone welcomed them, they brought
their poems, the young the old paying their
respects to Maj Ragain. We all cut the wedding
cake and hugged each poet and said hello.

Fuck the politicians and the ads
for pills to help us loose 30lbs.
We need to boil our water, eat grass
and rediscover the honesty of poetry, to
study the Russian Revolution, making sure
we have enough hot water for a bath.
You want something to write about,
watch a woman take her stockings off,
say something to get slapped hard.
Take a Ricksha back in time to witness
the birth of classical music, breathe
in those moments of inspiration,
tell me what it was that made men
betray everything sacred for love,
and this will be our secret.

Every river empties into the Jawbone,
    this *Church of the Backyard Poetry*
occupies just enough space for a good
story to stretch out, little wafers of poetry
offered under a tent set ablaze by metaphor,
the soapy faces, the little dream inside us,
as one by one we declare,
I was born again at the Jawbone.

Vlad,
  A Jawbone book for you.
  Thanks for bringing your
  bucket of fire to the
  Jawbone, your poems, your
  passion.
                    Maj

I am the Professor Emeritus
of holding the hands of my friends
who want to commit suicide.
Together we scream out to the world,
give the violins away to the gypsies.
Remember history,
the great purges,
when everything but our madness
was thrown into the bon fires.
One poem whispering in our ear...
rushing from room to room,
those months apart wetting our appetite,
only to find our lover in the bedroom
already making love to someone else.
This is what is written in the notebooks
and read out loud at the Jawbone.

There's the Kentucky Derby, free food,
pastries made by incredibly kind people,
hey! where are the pig-knuckles?
We started to read the poetry
of Yehuda Amichai, Yusef Komunyuakaa,
Robert Creely, Lucille Clifton, Gerald Stern
and Bukowski over and over again.

159

They came, Steve Abbott, Wendy Shaffer,
Carly Sachs, Georgiana Eckles, Al Milburn,
poets that will never get published,
poets young enough to still love hard and
work the third shift, living on next to nothing,
not ashamed to tell the world that all their
possessions fit inside a sandwich bag.
e.b. bortz, Sandy Hazley, Ben Gulyas,
Lisa Citore, Alice Cone I could kiss you,
Katie Daley, Ben Rader, Brian Taylor,
poets who looked for arrowheads only
to find a naked sky, the half-folded earth
teasing with bits of brick, the old faith
of dull shinny pennies without dates.
Adam Brodsky, Maggie Anderson, Merle,
David Thornberry, Kathy Korcheck,
just a partial record of the voices.

It Was Vladimir Swirynsky
at Brady's Café who turned the world
upside down, rejection slips falling from
the rafters, unexpected like a sudden May
snow storm, like a Sharon Olds sex poem.
The hell with all those editors we were
falling in love again, writing without fear
and those nasty rejection notes
falling...falling...falling on our heads.
We kept mailing out our best because
failure is our eternal partner.

On a Friday night some kid
quoted a line from Ginsberg's *America,*
I smoke marijuana every chance I get.
    I being the cruel mother just laughed,
being the coy mistress of wisdom kept
my thoughts to myself.
The Jawbone had its share of madmen
shouting to the tent rocks of Kasha-Katuwe,
this is all bullshit, too many words about nothing.
Only they knew about life and death,
had climbed Mt. Everest.

I am the associate professor
of how America raised its beautiful sons
to let them die in Vietnam, of two old people
who understand the language of flowers,
of office girls who can only hear
the sound of the surf while locked up
in the corporate attics of profit,
of falling asleep on the couch with my
shoes on and the traffic lights coming
alive as beautiful young women
who stop all the traffic.

I am at the Jawbone again, saluting the
voices, the soup kitchens, every stranger
I ever met on the highways who had
too much to say about nothing.
Especially that one time in Winslow Az
when a tough old broad cornered me,
Hey mister, would you like a cup of coffee
and listen to some cowboy poems?
The coffee was really bitter but that little
shake-n-bake sure had a way with words.

There Is So Much Poetry

that some of us have gone mad,
on a whim cheat death with bizzare stunts
that leave us in wheelchairs,
      fame—something we hunger
      for but are not fed.

We place a propeller beanie
on our head, apply subtle
pressure to our ego, fall in love
again and again with our corduroy
trousers, the mere touch of the fabric
the next best thing to haiku heaven.

Gnomes freak us out, we bend
the rules, fight fire with fire,
crowd under the mistletoe with
every member of the Bombay
bicycle club hoping for a kiss.
As a thousand suns audition to hold
hands with the earth, women write
ordinary poems, words begging
us to do extraordinary things.

We want our poems
to assume a degree of risk,
to open every crack
in the universe,
to have consequences
beyond this world.

On rare occasion
a stroke of genius
works its way loose,
we stare into the sun,
acquire a clarity
that places us on a mountain
in Tibet to overhear
            the words...
  *You're looking but
  you're not seeing.*

Unwavering we ignore
the obvious and continue
to write and embarrass
our contemporaries.

Footsteps In The Woods

for Mom

If I was in the woods for an hour the lost
secrets of ancient civilizations would
set up traps for me—

Armed with half a sandwich and a pocket knife
I searched for dinosaur eggs, too many times
would hear sobbing in the woods, walking
past ash-dust green moss on the sides
of trees that looked too much like ghosts,
the faces of murdered Jews.

The world was moving backwards, in times of
peace there are more wars then one can imagine,
opium clouds casting a shadow over hillsides
and cities, girls in the sixth grade with this sense
of urgency, breaking curfew to become women.
It was Little Red Riding Hood that
I was afraid of, not the wolf.

I became a headhunter, a cult classic,
a super hero about to get his own comic book.
All summer I kept looking, hoping to find
a sketchbook filled with the names of the lost,
a picture of my mother wearing a winter scarf,
who barely escaped from the Germans who
were steadfast in trying to shorten her life.

Love is too much
of a glamorized metaphor,
a wooden ship with sails, winds
blowing like the wishes of small boys.
We can't stop the death, the madness
so we save our pennies, help out
by washing the dishes, avoiding
strangers who want to kiss
our foreheads.

We can do nothing,
out of frustration we sneak
out the back door, running down
the streets leaving behind fresh tracks
of our sorrow 'til someone grabs
a hold of us, someone who's willing
to love us, like the gods breathing into
us the first breath. Suddenly we feel
the weight of the oceans, the heart
wanting to love the world back.

Loud Knock

A knock on the door,
keeping quiet
becuase I know
who's there,
don't want
to hand out
any more
change.

After a few
minutes it's back
to pretending
I'm a writer,
baseball game
on the radio,
I put the pencil
down, listening
is more important
now.

Once I got
to bat in a little league
game, I bounced my bat
on home plate,
swung at the first
pitch with
my eyes closed.

It's a long season,
but in the middle
of an inning I'll
fall in love with
the game again,
bare feet touching
tall grass, a foul
ball reaching
the seats,
someone with
a fat cigar
makes a great
catch.

A batter strikes
out, the crowd
wanting another
home run,
and I think
how lucky
I was to see
a no hitter,
for at least one
week owned
a Mickey Mantle
rookie card,
and a Willie Mays
who robbed us
in the '54
World Series.

Faith

I have no voice but when I need
to cry or laugh.

I have no heart but when
someone needs to be loved.

I have no need of faith except when
the earth sings the song of end times.

When darkness crowds out the sun,
non-believers profess they never strayed.

When everyone has a finger pointed at them,
our grief, our tears labeled as second hand joy,

it is indeed a beautiful day as we turn our backs
to the Devil's gate, march as though we have

won the battle, only to return to the valley of the
lost, an empire of ignorance that we have built,

a race of giants without
faith...

First Mondays - Hotel Alcazar

For years I searched the attic
hoping to find the blue pages of my
lost manuscript, the dreams
and toils of a thirteen year old boy.
I must confess at the moment
I'm trying to stay awake
at the hotel Alcazar, a small fee
paid to watch and listen to a play.
A beautiful place, built in 1924,
elegant thin wooden doors,
the chairs and women too close.
Not one of these creatures
is wearing oxford pumps or even
thinks of wearing a colorful fedora.
They own the look, flaunting their
perfect tan of wealth, so easily
erasing me from the room.
They know their herbs and have trained
their husbands to live their lives
without the honey of bad language.
After the performance we file out,
I want to start a conversation but
what could possibly hold their
attention for more than a minute?

The Quiet Ocean of Regrets

On Venice Beach a large bent compass
needle points to a better world, a call comes
from my daughter, something about being
stuck, transmission problems,
I explain, *sweetheart I'm in California.*
She doesn't want me to fall in love again,
says I'm too old for jogging, it's as though
I died years ago, my life a failure.

I am dealing with everyone's harmless lies,
tasting salt water, convinced a barrel of oil
is worth more than a dozen beautiful faces.
Here, the people tend to their organic
gardens, swallow multi-colored pills,
point to burning ships on the rooftops.
On the beach strangers offer to pour fresh
goat's milk on my cornflakes, wanting to
sell me what I left behind for five bucks.

Birdwatching through a Dollhouse Window

The years are topsoil,
the baby boomers over grazers.
Hey! I did my part, wrote some poems
in the 90's, witnessed the introduction
of even more bad poetry read out loud
in coffee shops, a staple
crop of angst for patrons who gave
this art form a deservedly thumbs down.

After a reading, I told the crowd
my next poetry book is titled:
Birdwatching and wondering why on
earth was I cursed with this large
and crooked nose and why did
I kiss a sixty-five pound Asian Carp
and send the picture to Southern
Poetry Review with the caption,
"We drank Wild Turkey 'til
the music stopped and we listened
for the laughter of despair, the black
spoon of night naked, vulnerable
like nobility without a nightshirt.
I smoked my last cigarette and walked
back to the car wearing the one shoe
I did't throw into the blue eyed river.

Tracy Lyn Rottkamp

Where are you, editor supreme who
underlined love in her letter and wanted
to publish everything I wrote.
      Where are you and the others,
        all of us having an *Affair Of The Mind,*
          sweetheart I'm still writing poetry.

Tracy, tell me you haven't grown old,
that you still want me to mail out my bio.
I have great news, 13 is the new 18,
50 is the new 30, facebook the new truth.
There was a post on the internet,
whatever happened to that crazy girl from
New York state.
I've tried to find you and Kathy,
but there are no new poems,
what have the men done to you.

Last Night

was my birthday,
I would tell you something
about the day but nothing
happened of interest,
the hours but a gaping hole
to be filled with pity,
of watching the birds
on the front lawn
who came to pray,
of reading about
the extinct ivory-billed
woodpecker,
of laughing about
the importance of voice
as pure fiction,
this graduate who
recieved her literary degree
about to become part
of the mustang round up,
listen—
the heart is hard at work
writing happy endings, busy
opening up birthday cards
with little scribbles that
bring smiles to our faces.

Brasier - Brassiere

definition: a brassiere is an
undergarment that covers, supports,
and elevates the breasts.

Watching—
almost an hour spent watching you fuss
with your new pretty white laced bra.

   Adjusting the cups up front,
re-adjusting the straps in the back,
   adjusting the cups up front,
re-adjusting the straps in the back,
   adjusting the cups up front,
re-adjusting the straps in the back,
   adjusting the cups up front.

Still, it doesn't seem to fit you.
at my urgings you try the black one
and the process starts over again.
Your breasts two islands that I swim
between, slowly crawling up on shore
to hear the drums of the uprising,
painting my face so I can get close
enough to dance around the fire.

UNEARTHLY

They were curious,
      listening to the sounds of tugboat
      Sally Ann nudging the world
      towards a hopeful peace,
yet somewhat careful since our solar system
was designated as an Elephant crossing.
      With no coin of exchange,
      they passed up great deals like
      six for a dollar post cards.

President Eisenhower make a deal with
the space aliens, details are sketchy but it had
something to do with all the fish in the oceans.
They didn't know anything about golf,
couldn't improve his game, later screwed up
Jimmy Carter by having him lust for peace.

They came to watch the movies
at the drive-ins, hot dogs and popcorn
dancing in high heels made them zoom
and zig-zag through the atmosphere
during intermission.
At night they would follow old jalopys
on desert roads, put a straw into our skulls
to find out our names. Those little shits
with their ray guns, dysfunctional
orel cookie heads after getting tired
of chasing slow jets decided to have
some fun with our cattle.

Someday I'll be driving the roads
late at night, flipping the FM dial,
up ahead red, blue, green lights
flashing like a tow truck about to yank
a few of us off this planet, work gloves
on, going about their business
like they own the heavens.

Sometimes the smallest of possibilities
crashes in to us unxpectedly,
the mind spinning like a saucer
on a string in a 50's sci-fi epic.

To Have Written Poetry

There's no shame in being poor
or in disliking people, the public
which has no interest in your prose,
wanting only to see blood as in all the
pages that chronicle those small details
about your miserable life that
they read over and over again.
How they love failure—
their own as they try to impress
everyone at parties by quoting
Wallace Stevens and Thomas Hardy.

There's no shame in knowing just
one language and trying to write
in tongues or wearing our winter coat
because we don't own a spring jacket.

Even if this makes no sense
it's true, never trust the poeple
who borrow what you don't have
making you feel that you own
even less of what you don't have.

The roof leaks,
pictures on walls moved around,
news of cars crashing into poles,
reports of fog as though it was a living thing.
You have to have been in
love to write poetry.

Sitting at the typewriter at 3:14am
hungry men wait in the parking
lot of Home Depot, the lucky ones
to labor for a day with a roofing crew.
And so it is with life,
we continue to sleep with strangers
who don't believe in angels,
the coffee and light switch
not worth a kick in the ass.

Paradise

Moving mountains of coal by hand,
laborers load boxcars for a dollar a day.

A handyman (that my neighbor says
can't be trusted) is under the car
about to replace the fuel pump.
He has an interpreter with him,
utters two words during the whole day.
The last of my meager savings
and all of the first place poetry prize
money will be handed over to him.
It's a hot day, I'm trying to write a haiku
about silvered aspens covered in snow.
Sitting on the front steps it's become
obvious that roof and gutters need repair,
next to me a five pound bag of dry
cat food that mama cat won't touch—
Stranded in a dying neighborhood,
a dying city,
lots of ants crawling inside
a milkshake container,
I'll trade my paradise
for theirs.

Brief History Of Coming To America

Not far from Jersey Shores I find out
that the streets are not paved with gold,
not knowing the language and much too young
declined to wear the crown of spoken word hipster.

I'm sure I stood for a moment,
a beggar of sorts, the mind outstretched as
some passer by smiled to reassure me
that one day I would be back.

Kerouac just down the street, as luck would
have it I found a winged horse and didn't
travel down that road.

Bookstores

In the old days there was no flavored coffee,
bottled water, just lots of books stacked
two feet high on steps leading
to a second floor or a poorly lit basement.
Life and Saturday Evening Post just
a few of the magazines kept in hand-made
bins to be had for a quarter.

Two for one paperback and comic book
exchange policies kept the stores crowded on
Saturday afternoons. It was at Kay's Bookstore
that I parted with Journey into Mystery #83, the
first issue and origin of Thor for ten cents.

Decades later I'd read my poetry in these
stores all over the country when people actually
appreciated you being there, offered to buy your
books. They would buy you a cup of coffee,
tell you something interesting about themselves.

On the Gulf Coast or Miami Beach how dearly
I miss those smiles, the casual dress of women.
I payed my way by selling 8 x 10 prints of the
Three Stooges, John Wayne, Marilyn Monroe
and others. I managed to survive the days from
the good will of people and new friendships.
From a Walt Whitman poem, *I celebrated myself,*
roller skated fearlessly on the beach bike paths
guided by the lamplight of the cosmic surf.

St. Stanislaus Church

The week after Easter and Jesus is still
on the cross, an accident of faith
has brought me here.
A two year old boy fidgets around
with goldfish crackers in one hand
the other trying to touch a white Lilly.
He leaves the pew to investigate
a newborn across the isle, we watch
with approving smiles as our hearts
turn into the longhand of joy.

Those of us sitting in the back rows wait
for the collection basket holding our
humble offering. Some of us wondering
if we have made men and saints
holier than they are.
We say a little prayer for loved ones,
for the raging dark clouds
that remind us of death.
Outside the world is still the same,
weeds growing from the cracks of sidewalks,
a parade to begin shortly on Fleet Avenue.
Grace hands me a paint brush expecting
me to change the world into the beauty
we imagine it once was.

Heroes Of The City

Hal Jordan is the
Green Lantern and I'm a fool,
odds on favorite to be the
the misfit at the bus stop,
a designated looser at any
given party.

Another wasted day waiting
for work at the Temp agency
to call in for workers, for
someone to come in needing
to fill up the company van
with day laborers.

You hear about people breaking
their teeth on soft bread, listen to
the rhetoric of old men who haven't
shaved since the Hale Bopp comet,
filth on the clothes,
losing lottery tickets crumpled
up like a sickness inside purses.
All these people, all of us
so certain that things are not
going to get better, skid row
lipstick neutral beauties,
whores to be had for
a couple of beers or less.

I start up a conversation with one
of these, *get used to it honey, this*
fat ass is only gonna get bigger
women, but I'm not crazy enough
to hold her attention, she can tell that
I don't drink, I'm a nerd for beleiving
in honesty, the free paint program.
Same same as everyone else,
a zero of the streets,
watchmen of the lost
change on the sidewalks.

We are the beaten-down-store
front-church heroes of the City.
We are the faces of the new
enemy, a large segment
of the great recovery,
store for rent   - not hiring
space for lease - not hiring
building for sale - not hiring
We are heroes of the city betting
fifity dollars to win twenty-five,
betting two hundred to win
one hundred and
so it goes on and on...

There are worse
things than begging
for money—
one of them is not begging
or asking for a handout.

Thor has his hammer,
Iron-Man his armour,
Sub-Mariner his little wings,
what do we have—
the religion of an empty
rusted out green canteen,
the three page poem that
insures our cult-figure status,
hard luck stories of floods,
songs of those tired souls picking
the riches coffee beans in the world,
pawn shops burndend with magic rings,
garbage day bonanza picnics,
the long-out-of-print oversized X,
a symbol that rarely leads
us to the secret location
of a buried treasure.

The mind is nothing more
than a poorly lit room,
a Carl Barks story unfolding
at a lesurely pace,
a small town murder
that never sees print.

Another day at the office—
clocked out, car won't start,
hood latch broke,
tow truck man says
thirty minute wait,
forty in cash to pick
up my heap of junk.

Still, most of us had a good run
at life, got lucky with romance,
the years filling closets with nameless
things, filling boxes with red tag specials,
stores going out of business because
the two of us never came in to buy
anything during clearances.
We loved the bargains,
the salesmen who tried their
best to sell us something,
we outlasted them,
saved up a little money
in a jewelry box that got stolen
when they busted out
a basement window.

Still, we thought we would
make it to the finnish line, this
amazing race, the struggles that
brought you in then barely
out of a black hole.
I am thankful for my stubbornness,
thankful for writing so much—
lucky nobody bothered to read
that stuff, thankful for all the
times you smiled, your kisses
that came so dangerously
close to surrendering all the
secrets a man ever
wanted to know.

Early morning, making
the water run to the park,
empty gallon jugs
and bottles all over the floor,
looking right,
looking left,
nobody around, good,
one more week of
washing, another week
of living in solitude,
touching the whiteness of bone,
praying to a false god to remove
the good humor I'm wearing
as a mask to fool myself.

A man can only write
so much about the misfortune
he has created,
can only write so much
about what has disappeared
into the darkness forever
before the shadows claim
the heart, the only messenger
that kept telling me to write.

Miles From Nowhere

On old route 66
we stop for refreshments,
the desert an unlocked tool shed
full of smuggled accountant bones.
To prove to the world that we're
all insane somebody in the back
seat yells out,
Hey, Hey! I'm your monkey.
We're good at forgetting names,
believing that John Lennon & Yoko
pledged to each other to be no less
than painted flowers on canvass.
A bus load of movie stars stops
at the Church of the Stubbed Toe,
a peep show called night sky.
In a few hours we'll be at
Burning Man to build a rainbow
bridge to Asgard.
We are blessed with conviction
and enough household goods
to start a sculpture for peace.
After sunset old fires of love whisper
the names of four-legged gods,
first light to find us washing
our faces with dirty rags.

New Poems

A Matter of Balance

for r a Washington

I'm sitting here
eslaved by the perpetual
darkness,
the loafs of bread in revolt,
over-indulging themselves
on the colors of green and blue,
my prayers, Yeha-Noha—
wishes for happiness
go unanswered.

The only company that
comes over is the uninspired
poetry sent to me,
the manuscripts showing
off their false smiles,
limping around the room
without mentioning, or caring
that the earth is mother heart.

I want disturbing images,
an unforgettable fire,
the rib cage of Ethiopia
splitting wide open.

In a couple of days I'll
be reading at Snoetry 4
hosted by r a Washington
(one of my brothers in spirit)
in his little place called,
Guide to Kulchur.

Off course *Virginia* the world
is full of desperate people.
I have tried to rise above it,
maintain a balance by listening
to some healing Chinese flute music,
respecting Apache sacred spirits,
> chanting—
> reaching out to the First Nations,
> shatter open my skull,
> pour the wine of madness.

Eyes closed,
I feel the coming rebellion.

At the senior center a ninety year
old woman born in Jonestown
Guiana is wearing large silver butterfly
earnings, they are frozen in time
in a dream catcher,
to awaken after 82 days
in April to tell us that one
person can change the world.

What happened was while
at Edgewater park watching
the sunset, reaching out for what
a thought was the moon
I lost my balance and fell into
the empty hours of two autumns,
three winters of amnesia.
I'm sure I remembered having
a secret I wanted to devulge,
living in a small town where
songs from the rainforest
could be purchase for a nickel
at the cookie store.

Anyplace Is A Good Place

for Marian Anzalone

I don't think I will ever be able
to love a song more than this one—

Once I was king of the playground,
felt the vibration of honesty, sounds
of a distant train whistle that distracted
me from what I really wanted—
I am here now wanting
to touch your hair,
explain that the impossible
is but a distant garden.

Nothing feels right—
the tongue-pierced lost stars
crash through the roof of the world
like an endless chain of forgotten bands.
I'm out of control, stepping out in my
Ellington wing tip grain/rust suede shoes
to become your roadblock,
dying, lying, dying to own you—
to become your Paris.

Come tomorrow crowded trains
& street lights will greet the sunrise
in far off Istanbul, all I have,
is a thousand years of peace
in my pocket to offer you.

How is it that the blue October
of our desires became a runaway
train crashing into the hard
prayers of December?

I am Kansas, a broken down Buick,
like you dragged by some invisible
force, on life's hastily built raft
following the curvature of illusion.
I find myself on a ship of fools
with nothing but a hurried
sketch of your beauty that memory
tempts me with. I swear you
are the Cape of New Hope,
a last minute pardon.

      Let it rain over me….
I've seen this all before—
the streets of Calcutta flooded,
wooden statues and sacred debris
washed down to the ocean
like nostalgic pieces of the Berlin wall.
     Marian, take a closer look—
I'm the one balancing a Singer
sewing machine on my head
(my only means of income)
waist deep in thoughts about you.

Each hour is a century
full of inventions betraying
the goodness of humanity,
what saves us from the chaos
is holding hands, your smile
that is the center
of all that is rare and true.
Any place is a good place for us
to hide so you can show off your
guns N roses tattoo,
our first kiss to be practiced
like an unbroken promise,
as though our piano teacher
was yelling, demanding perfection.
By the time we figure out today
tomorrow will already be here,
will I be gone?
I am the foolish one,
nurturing a stubborn world
that insists that everything
about you
is like an unexpected
gift to unwrap.

To Cross The River
for Zenon

My brother just back from the first Gulf War
didn't seem right. I thanked him for the rug
and trinkets he had sent me, for not telling
me about the horrible details of death.

I was in a different war, still waiting to come back
home. Remember old Municipal Stadium, the
Beatles in 1965, the terrible beauty of innocence.
Which one of us crossed the river to find safety?

The cruel heart resurrects the sonnet moon,
the black widow loose in Russian, and they say
not far from here a murder of crows, the silence
between us that neither wanted or anticipated.

You're still marking off days on your Snoopy
short timer's calendar, looking at the photos
of depleted uranium shells, the little girl playing,
matters not if her name was Nafisah or Az-zabra.

Most disturbing is the truth, the cold ashes
of blasphemy, *there is nothing wrong with you*.
They didn't care if I liked westerns, John Wayne
& Jimmy Stewart, *have some coffee, it's free*.

Forget about fixing vending machines, we still
have a war to fight, reclaim that better future.
For years I've wanted to go back to Japan, visit
Saihoji Temple to find my lost love, will you help?

Boyd Funeral Home

She recalls
Mr. Boyd standing
over the casket
and taking out
his handkerchief
and gently
wiping off the
rain drops...

Listen—I Tell You Something

1.

Manhattan,
72nd Street, while doing
some work in a recording studio
one would eventually get thirsty
and walk out to the lobby.
There was a machine
that dispensed cans of beer.
Perched on top was a parrot (a sign
which read *Watch Your Fingers)*
who was trained to open
the can for those who wanted
bragging rights

2.

As much as one can love New York
City I left because no one was listening
to me. I left because all the joys & sins
of the wild and loud Russian immigrants
& the summer heat took its toll.
The kitchen alive with our nervous laughter,
the sharp knife of fiction finds you—
Cher blows you a kiss, being the person
she is invites you to a private party.

3.

At the Cleveland Metro Park Zoo
I'm greeted by three bitchy veterinarian
interns who were given boots & shovels
for the summer, introduced to the opera
of the absurd. The world perceived
me as an accomplished musician—
headpiece on, how is it the jackhammer
makes impossible demands of us,
how is it we escape impending disaster?

No one told me the pygmy
hippopotamus wasn't let out—
kept inside because of his bad temper,
my ass pressed against the rail
as I loosened the stubborn concrete.
I heard the faint sound of doom,
the confessions of empty rooms,
in an instant, stood up—
reached back to discover
I had no pants pockets.
That night I whispered *thanks*
to the twin sisters of luck.

Gypsy Beans & Baking Co.
for Gina, Amanda, Michelle

*We keep slaying our small dragons,
as the big one waits.*

February 21,
the slow deliberate sore feet
dance of below zero wind
chills are over,
the snow has melted,
it's more of an act than living
out the Amerikan dream,
a one-hit wonder.

This story,
this poem doesn't begin
or end here at Gypsy's
Beans & Baking Co.
I waundered off the streets
to show them the three dimes
I found on the sidewalk.

There are real people here,
Detroit Avenue working class
residents, an occasional lost soul,
not your typical high rise,
high times, high tech,
sorry I spilled my glass
of wine lobster fest crowd.

A young lady with a blue
Panamanian cloth purse with wolfs
on it catches my attention, the over
priced Moscow latte with raspberry
and white chocolate that's
probably worth a try.

The clocks on the wall
are broke—
4:32 PM Tibet,
7.23 AM in Madrid,
9:10 PM Cleveland,
somewhere a clue
that predicts within
a minute the moment
of our mass extinction.

There's a heroin, cocaine
epidemic in Cleveland,
all of Cuyahoga county,
northeast Ohio,
people dying,

Such is our happy lives,
    sons-of-bitches
    they got their due—
    that eternal meat grinder
    in the sky,

The world won't leave me alone,
Holly, two doors down tells me she
has blood poisoning, complains
there's too much of too little
that's happening. She lives with
someone who helps out with
the rent but never says a word.
I put my trust in Wonder Woman,
Diana Prince spinning
        in fast circles—
each episode a free
lay-a-way plan for
the lusting heart.

Newsflash:
7:08 in the morning/
a woman calls to invite me for
coffee and some French toast/
I don't want to go, writing
is the only thing that
has kept me out of trouble/
I tell her I'll be ready
in thirty minuites/

Julia has given me an expensive
baabaazuzu wool vw tote bag,
I've asked her to
watch *The Red Violin,*
the film and her are remarkable.
I feel compelled to tell her that
I'm almost a civilized man,
but the best I can do today
is be a mean face looking
out a car window.

This snowy February afternoon
paradise is a clumsy beast falling
down the stairs.
Just off the rapid I board a bus
by the West Side Market and two
young girls straight out of the book
of lost things (the night circus that
offers us the glitz & 25 cents peepshow
called sadness) get on with me.

They are just girls, barely pre-teen
Bettie Page wannabes—
wearing retro black tennis shoes,
things from their mother's dresser,
nothing more terrible and beautiful
as they take their clothes off,
Nazi death camps shoulder blades
highlighted and held in place
by a thin pick bra strap,
      showing off their bad boy blues,
      melted ice cream breasts.

What is wrong with them,
what's wrong with me?

The world has a special offer today,
a serious moment for us,
gets ready to hum in C minor—
      Soda pop
      Lollypop
      Sponge Bob
      Square Pants
      Beetle Bug
      No Hit Backs

I am 65,
I am thirteen,
do they know I'm a werewolf,
half-cocked, kinky,
every issue of *Painted Bride Quarterly*
showcasing one of my poems.

The Burning Bush Evangelical
Ministries van pulls up next to us,
we look at each other,
I could use a free meal,
but I'm not getting off—
better that my heart stabs itself
with the names of missing children,
that I keep an eye out
for these two helpless goldfinchs,
that they live long enough
to count all the stars.

> *Maybe you'll like it,*
> *comeon give me some more.*

The enemy we're
   all hiding from—
         the simple truth.

I think of Gina, Amanda, Michelle
who were in that hell hole only three
and a half blocks from my house.
On occasion I was on my bike just
two doors down on Seymour Avenue
doing some meaningless shit.

And I think to myself,
what a wonderful world.

In place of that house is a small
empty park, a flash of peacefulness
that I've walked in, some shrubs,
expensive flowers planted.
The powers to be want
us to forget, by any means
neccesary they dumb us down.

The little boy in me doesn't
understand the world anymore,
it has lost its beauty,
I have to teach the sidewalk
to stay out of the street.

I have to find that something
that's searching for me.

Later that evening James Crawford
of the Lakewood Library drives me
to Kent, Ohio for a poetry reading
(a posthumous book release of poetry
by Mort Krahling). He hands me a
556 page Bukowski book as a gift,
>   makes
>   me
>   read
>   a poem.

We stop in at Ray's for a bite,
endure the loud music, focus our
attention on the beautiful women,
The Pleasures of the Damed.
I'm afraid to tell him that
the child-like poems in my head
are the only friends I have.

It is at the Last Exit Books store
that we listen as Christopher Franke
stands up, "The last few days that
Dorothy was seriously ill I had this pain,
(places his hand near his heart)
that didn't go away until she died."

I give him a hug—
no words spoken,
this is part of the meaning
of life, our gorgeous yet feeble
effort of escaping from
tomorrow, coming to terms.

Tales Told Twice

Before I caught my toe in the mouse trap,
before my father hid behind his car as his

bride fired two shots at him I thought the
world perfect. In the quiet community

of Broadview Heights we had a fire going
every night, roasting hot dogs. Wearing

his rattlesnake boots the renter played
his guitar, sang and told his stories. Seems

he and Glen Campbell would run into each
other out west, he was the better player,

had the best voice, not for bad luck he'd
be the one on tv, pulling in the big bucks.

I believed him—let my hair grow long,
that summer penciled in my one and only

birdie on a par 5. Precisely for no reason
at all hanged himself on my dad's property.

A new renter moved in who couldn't sing
or dance but paid the rent on time.

Stereotype - a Rough Draft

1.

There's no place like this...
metaphors joyfully squeezed
out of a tube of toothpaste,
the furniture stolen from
various second-rate motels.

This emerald isle I've created
is nothing short of spectacular,
magic marker profanity
on the walls that's appropriate
for all ages, worthy of any
auction house catalog,
countless garbage bags full of clothes
stacked in the nose cone
of the closet.

On every wall many photographs
of four lane highways, fast cars that
got 12 mpg, including a green Dodge
Charger which I playfully butchered
up the gears & stalled out
in a Detroit dealership show room.

2.

I was the whimsical DP,
the protagonist jumping
fences to escape
the neighborhood bullies.
The not so hidden treasure
were the bottles of *coca-cola*
to be had for a dime
at the Texaco station.
Back then gasoline was
twenty-eight cents a gallon,
the pay phones spotless and in
working order, honest!

You might think this is all
made up, that none of it's true,
let me tell you something...
truth is warm to the touch,
a paper-mâche mask
we wear to debunk the myth
of white priviledge.

3.

If anyone bothers to ask
my weakness is watching re-runs
of the Muppet show, putting twenty
to win on three lgged long shots.
      Enough, enough—
I bash my head against the wall
so you may know that home made
pies have mysterious origins,
that stealing silverware
is a form of artistic creativity.

Somewhere in the critics notebook
our poems become a vacant lot,
we decide to become ad sales people
humming Day-o (the banana boat song.)
Like you I want to be kissed,
so the world will start wearing funny
clothes again. I take an oath to die
with a Russian smile on my face,
much to your surpise rush out
to piss on the wilting flowers.

Stranger in Paradise
for Lee Ann

But there is nothing here to harm you!
You are the first living creatures to ever come
from the great darkness. I want you to stay...
there is so much to talk about.

Close your eyes and I'll kiss you...
On the shelf are half full containers
of aspirin, a bottle of Foxhorn wine,
a Christmas mug never used, a blue bowl
with the bottom melted away.
Near by, on a pile of books the only
photo I have of a woman from Osaka.
I'm still riding the Bullet train,
looking out the window at Mt. Fuji
wondering if the words,
     Don't let go of me,
are seeds that I never planted.

I been in the noisy Garden of Eden,
learned to use chop-sticks, an embryo
floating in an ocean of mercy & kindness.
Today a kind soul gave me two Beatles
books. I didn't catch her name,
wanted to say, please stay—
there's so much to talk about.

Childhood Splendor

I'm stuck in no-man's land (whatever
that means) reaching for a small cup
of light and a copy of X-men.

Up for bid,
Two-Gun Kid issue #89,
Donald Duck 40's lighter,
spring action in working order,
insides gutted out, Johnny Mathis
song sheet. This is all that's left
after you peel away forty years
of empty cheerfulness & false hopes.

It's coming back to me,
the long summers, nose bleeds—
afternoons spent after school
at the A & P hustling groceries.
A pocketful of change
was enough to purchase
a bag full of comic books
at the local paperback
exchange store.

My parents didn't approve, told me
comics were created in the Devil's
workshop. Stuck in my makeshift
clay spittlebug world continued to put
trust in the six panels per page,
blood-ink, mutation or pure of heart—
heroes consumed by the disease of flesh,
the stories all too real,
Marvel's Fantastic Four defeating
Dr. Doom & saving the world.

At School I was preoccupied
with typing class, unaware that
my prom date would call off
the whole thing and humiliate
            me in front of the class.
I hadn't a clue on how
to become sophisticated or
what it took to be popular.
I still played like a little
kid in the streets
after a rain storm.

At sixteen I bought a car, answered
an ad in the back of a comic and made
five thousand dollars a month working
part time from the kitchen table.
On Monday's I'd sort out
the Sunday funnies (Tarzan, Prince
Valiant, Dick Tracy, Flash Gordon
from out of town papers at the largest
book store in town before they
were thrown out.

Something always found me
from out of the comic pages—
Sandman, Electro,
the Lizard, the quiet & insane
smile of the Joker coaxing
me to come out from under
the blanket.
The epic battle between
the Human Torch
and Iceman reminded
me of Robert Frost's poem,
Fire and Ice.

Ten cents allowed me
to buy a brand new comic
off the stands, it would be Donald
Duck the misunderstood hero,
that got the most laughs from me.
In Walt Disney's comics & Stories
#227 Junior Woodchucks set out
to prove their skills, that clever
old duck lowered by helicopter atop
a lighting blasted tree.
He outwits the young troopers,
in the end bad luck becomes
the indisputable winner.
A lot of evenings were spent
writing on the inside covers in
blue ink. *The world's greatest
comic collection*

I wasn't impressed with Magneto,
legendary provocteur and villain,
didn't care for his costume.
Dr. Octopus, Juggernaut, Stilt-man
were the villains to fear,
they were always busy passing
out medals to all us cowards.
Didn't the comic characters know
that to cure the effects from
radiation all they needed to do was
take baking soda and mix
it with sea salt.
I loved the stories of the haunted tank
in G.I. Combat, opened up the photo
album to glance at the life and times
of Scrooge McDuck.
Was there anyone stranger
than Mr. Mxyzptlk?

       Before the mutants take-over,
       my fellow earthlings....

We must find another planet,
begin civilization anew.

Strange Adventures,
Mystery in Space, five gorillas
playing basketball for the
championship of the galaxy,
the stories made more sense
than whatever I was learning
in school. It was Sgt. Rock & easy
company outwitting the nazi's,
it was Turok Son of Stone
trapped in an age of dinosaurs
with nothing but bow and arrow,
courage & honor that
always saved the day.

I grew older, started chasing
blonds and red heads, got lucky,
met a beautiful woman with
black hair like Vampirella's,
someone who could paint,
who didn't mind that I had three
hubcaps on the car.
From that point I built my little
empire, one wooden shelf
at a time to reclaim my
treasured childhood.

It was 1976, (trapped in a world
he never made) Howard the Duck
was running for president, in the
basement I set up campaign HQ, sold
presidential buttons for two dollars.
Seated in the rocking chair of
immaturity I plotted the
takeover of the world,
kept all my issues of Howard
the Duck #1's locked up.

Not having ever grown up
Bonnie Jean talked me
into selling it all.
Somehow I separated
from the world, the day to day
chit-chat between Archie,
Betty & Veronica.

I reach into my pocket
for twelve cents, for a flood
of memories of my first
wife passing out flyers
in her Supergirl outfit.

What is there to do now,
all the comics gone—
you're alone,
smiling as you look
at the old photos again,
her red cape lecturing
those of us not willing
to die for art or beauty.

Mimetolith

definition: A natural tropographic feature, rock
outcrop, rock specimen, mineral specimen or loose
stone the shape of which resembles somthing else.

The power of imagination,
   how to tell the birds from the flowers—
      the face on mars in the Elysium region,
fragments of bones from ancient oceans
form vertigo visions.

At the Natural History museum
a gimmick-free skeleton dinosaur
is about to wave back at us,
the elusive identity of the class
joker about to be revealed.

I have come back here as an adult
to patrol the exhibits rooted
in the gospel of fresh observations.
The days of being Turok,
dinosaur hunter behind me,
the secrets of Stonehedge but
a thrown away double-sized
issue of a Marvel comic.

Off in the corner next
to the saber tooth tiger
are a few rocks,
I squint and see more
faces than I could hope for,
echoes of godlike creatures
that eventually left a record
of their struggles.

Nature insistent, tries to coax
me back to reality—
telling me I'm not living in
the time of butterflies,
that I didn't have
breakfast with Buddha
this morning.

Hours later as I lean against
the wall, a rare delight,
the unexpected grace
of a rock being just a rock,
the stars nothing more
than apple seeds.

Sandusky Coffeehouse Reading
for Bill Wright

A good friend drives
me to Sandusky, Ohio
for a poetry reading.
I receive an envelope stuffed
with cash and a Mr. Smith's
Coffeehouse t-shirt that reads,
Make Coffee Not War.

It was here we celebrated
Bill's 97th birthday, listening
to his poems about
his beloved wife Chris,
our tears flowing freely.
Before leaving I shook
his hand shielding myself from
the sadness in his eyes.
All too quickly indulged myself
in self-pity, driving off in a rush
past the State theatre,
on the backseat dozens
of love poems I swore
I wouldn't write.

More than once I return and
read Denise Levertov's *First Love*,
Philip Levine's *The Return*
and quarantine myself
on a distant planet,
far from the wellspring
of my heartaches.

My father, immigrant—
mechanic, heavy coffee drinker
would take us on Sunday drives.
The appetizer, the thrill
was him speeding towards
an imaginary future of my own
making on a section of old
route 3 'til we got
to the custard stand.

I am rooted in the coffee bean,
the forgiveness of memory,
the poetry of a slow
unwinding morning.
Holding on to a pocket watch
five years now for her,
unwilling to decipher
her heart, her intentions.

Bill would need some help
getting to the microphone,
his voice soft, barely reaching
the first table in front of him.
How he would swim the years,
standing at attention like the old
soldier he was praising a love
more profound than any sermon
that ever reached my soul.

What words can I use,
what language to capture the ear,
what image to catch the eye,
what story to bring us to our
knees, the hunger that
can't be satisfied.

This quiet evening I spread jam
on a slice of brittle white bread,
can't recall the names
of Jupiter's moons.
I am lost in thought, so far
away from everything,
so close to nothing.

Half a Block That Way

This gate hangs well—and hinders none
refresh and rest—then travel on

Thank God for my cute ex-girlfriend,
for all those years of bliss despite her

ad nauseam complaining about my bad
habits, so compulsive in her cleanliness

I felt like a fidgetting cockroach in the
middle of a dance floor during a jitterbug

contest. Like most relationships (limited
time offer) she left leaving behind her

A.S.I.D. cloth handbag. It's the only
possession that I have that's worth

anything from all those woodpile and candy
kiss years. Call me crazy, my tote bag has

been a faithful companion, aiding me in
illegal acts of thievery. I embrace it like

a celebrated sculpture, hand washing it,
giving it a place of honor. Perhaps this

knapsack of words is worth a second
look, will show up in an obscure journal.

Tomorrowland
for Donna Voss

Seems you were the only one I noticed,
the girl who pointed at and wore a button
that proudly proclaimed,

> I'll BE THE ONE YOU
>   WON'T FORGET.—

We were once young, like drunken
Gods scaling the north face
of the impossible. Some of us worshiped
Mick Jagger, fancied crazy people
who pointed at & swore the moon
was a hidden bomb.

Ola Ritachka was the hot one—
short-skirted teacher, the one
who pulled the rug from under us.
We were handcuffed to history class,
to Beethoven, the unavoidable
age of miracles.

Cathy Wolf, a feminist of sorts
raised her hand in class
and said that no man could
offer a woman the world.
I felt a rubber ball in my hand,
the drift of bewildered continents,
my thumb squarely on the equator.
I looked for someone to throw it at.

We hardly raised our hands
in algebra or biology class,
unhooked the bras of girls who
believed they were ugly because
they wore glasses.

I write about the second winter,
the regrets, not having
asked you for a dance.

Lincoln High School, diploma
in hand I'm like a goat eating paper,
fearful of black Santa's,
the Osmonds and the floating
decimal point.

Donna invites me over
Wednesday night
to watch Star Trek in color.
We were parked near the zoo,
on a winding dirt road
that seemed to be full
of stalled out cars.

It was a novel-in-progress,
your kiss set off alarms.
The only dance is desire,
I felt the sweet sorrow
of your breats
and did nothing—

Global Warming

Ice capes have melted, water
rushing in to cover most of Florida.
Oranges fall off the trees,
rotting vegetables
become the new currency.
If only the extinct mastodons
understood the gravity of cause
and effect, they might of stolen
the promised bounty from us.

We were warned,
golf courses under water,
the muddy footpath
of *I told you so* piggybacked
on the news that New Orleans
has fallen back into the sky.

Press escape to continue
with your life.

I am on the on-ramp of panic,
headed for New York City.
Hoping to arrive there before
it disappears to become the mythology
of Atlantis, before they run out
of mustard at Coney Island.

Royal Street Blues

Singing, down inna bottom a da woirld

percolatin in our heads
are songs without words which
come pretty much from nowhere.
I was down in New Orleans
often before Katrina,
before the alligators
got their citizenship papers,
before I starting haggling
price with the prostitutes
and gathering up purple
beads as I followed
the Mardi Gras
floats to Canal Street.
Got me a good view
of the Mississippi,
got me some scuffed up shoes,
got me some pretty women
to pose for the camera.
It was at Jackson Square
I started out on my next great
journey, letting the music
mess me all up.

The Veiled Sky

We slowly become little fish
lost in the thin woods.

We walk the path
made up of two parts stone,
one part bamboo whispers.

Barefooted, we look around
for fallen fruit, never see
the punch line coming.

Susan Lynn

Each man kills the thing he loves

Dreams can be persuasive, you think
your father is alive, your bride
in the kitchen is a miracle of bones,
more of a prayer answered than a
question posed in *Scientific American*.
On the armrest of the couch three
photos, two are of my ex-wife in the
middle of an arts festival in Greenwich
Village, the other is of her as a young
woman balancing an armful of books.
In her twenty something days
honesty and beauty was the color
of her purposely wild Aztec
paper-flowered brushed hair.

I met her when she was a blond—
I am completely certain
that I am over her.
            The simple truth,
the first time she asked for a hug
life became a misspelled word,
love became the new world promised,

            suddenly the word you,
            meant YOU!

By way of Ellis Island I stumbled
into the saintly arms of a full-figured
woman, she could play the piano
and I of limited writing skills
dared to write her a love poem.
I was too old, too young,
all of forty-five and lost in
the uneasiness of being single,
the genius who inherited
everything he never wanted.

We would drive to Youngstown,
spend the night at aunt Marge's
house, church in the morning.
And I loved the sweetness of her
sweetness, the no nonsense
vodka, factory whistle laughter
and jazzed up hardwood floor sex.

The real winter hasn't arrived yet,
a car pulls up in front of the house,
I wait a minute then take
an early autumn morning walk.
The Ukrainian in me doesn't
understand why she left,
why I can't let go.

Small Town Dreams

Left by the side of the road
a burlap sack
full of the unknowing.
Then suddenly,
too easily,
the moon rises
to sit still on a fence post.

Thankfully hours before
we added eggs & bacon
& eight hours of sleep
to our shopping list.

You Rembember

One day last week
I misread down as drown
and ruined a beautiful story.

It's been cold all week.
I recall a blanket placed over
a body pulled from the sour
creaking waters of lake Erie.

There is the paperwork
to fill out—
notifying next of kin,
the sky walking
away from the clouds.

It is the silence that
explains nothing—
and it is in the tic-toc
and honesty of words
between friends that sorrow
enriches our lives,
gives meaning to that
faint distant glow.

New York City Deli

Every other day or so I'd walk
into the overpriced grocery store
for batteries or fresh vegtables
and would run into Tiny Tim.
He'd be wearing a smile-button blue
tuxedo with chocolate and strawberry
stains all over it, his head and upper
torso down inside the ice cream
freezer scooping up an armful
of ice cream bars and the like.

Rumor had it that in a warehouse
not far from here he kept over
one hundred thousand vinyl records
that he sold to pay all his bills.
I never spoke to him, too much
in a hurry to get back to writing
lyrics in a chicken-coop of a room
that needed a woman's touch,
her anger, the no cigarette
in fourteen hours, my cocky
insults that would add to her
frustrations, open a portal
of insightful honesty that
helped move the song along.

The First Steps off the Curb

as always it's the little words
that confuse me, darling

Being the indistinguishable professor
emeritus at Cleveland State University
I confess my love affair with run-on-
sentences, sneaking out late at night
to confront subject verb conflicts.

The Flying Fish Cafe is my favorite
hangout, it's here I do the
Daffy Duck double talk, watch
girls behaving like boys and hand
them my business card.

I bow to the of and to and sometimes
why of my misguided students—
    tell them of the joys of climbing
    a mountain, of having sex
    in an elevator.

I was a child prodigy, memorized
half of the phone book. A recluse who
sometimes joined the gang outside
to play hop-scotch, skinned my sissy
white knees for the sins of the world.

Suicide

I admire beauty from a distance,
too timid to get close to the turth
or much less a pure heart,
searching for the courage
to shout out, to risk all I have
for the sake of justice.

This is a poem that busts down
the doors of the Cleveland Museum
of Art, spray paints in all the glory
of the rightious on a Monet
painting the words—
   Don't forget about me.

I'm asking Elizabeth Bishop,
Emily Dickerson to transfer,
to enfuse the kindness of their souls
so I might defuse my anger.

I have a daughter, she is smiling,
she is alive, I'm sending out a search
party to find the Ghost Rider,
saluting the bewildered flag of faith
that's planted firmly in our memories.

After It Rains
for Tina

After it rained
all night three mice
had to row across
the kitchen floor
in an empty
noodles box.

After it rained last night
someone fired some
shots outside.
I felt alone—
misery is but a petty thief
so I dragged myself back
into the rented room of sleep,
back into the pages,
the light traffic of a dream
that's found an all night diner,
a smiling waitress that's
penciled you in as the
special of the day.

A Human Interest Story

It use to be so cool smoking
a cigarette after sex, letting your
partner know, the world that it was
High Noon, and you had just shot
the sheriff. No one was safe now,
you— looking around with a half-smile
letting the ladies know of your *under
the hood, everything checks out
ok, wash the window* intentions.

Thinking back to the first job
I had after high school,
eavesdropping on a conversation
between some older workers,
a man complained that his red headed
wife only had sex in the morning.
No matter what he did or tried night
time meant a quiet evening at home.
I thought how awful his situation.
But now being older and wiser
I realize it doesn't matter what
time of day or night that someone
hands you a million dollars—
    you just gladly accept it.

The best story was told
to a group of us young boys
with instructions not
to tell anyone else.
He was over six feet tall,
on the plus side of 200 lbs.
& proud of his beer belly.
It was bed time, the lights out,
about to do the deed when
his wife heard some noises
& asked him to investigate.
Upset with the timing
of all this he rushed
out of the room without
thinking, his penis still
wide-eyed and trustworthy
plunged into a shopping cart.
The thrill ride was over—
thank you Odin,
I laughed 'til the sun
fell into the branches
of a flat lake.

Polka Dots & Moonbeams

The moon is an empire
of craters, the senseless
God of obedience.
On the dark side factories,
a giant furnace of molten
lead pouring out little
Buddha statue curiosities,
an endless line
of American doughboys,
the stuff of boyhood
dreams.

As we grow older
the stories get lost,
we trip over contradictions,
mumble, *Inka Dinka Doo,*
second-quess if there
are human footprints
on the Moon.

Korea - Observation Post
for Glenn Eure

The ghost of it whimpered back last night
from a cold November 50 years ago."

Somehow you endure the *things*
of this world, the clearness of winter,
half-moon your only eyes.
Bless the good earth, the black
boot frozen hand sticking
up through the half-finished
grave like an apology.

The fingers curled, a cup holder
for your coffee, a distraction from
the imagined stray bullet with your name
etched on it. I have talked to those
troubled souls, men who only nod their
heads, the broken English of silence
that's an outcry wanting to explain
what we can't begin to understand.

War is a dull knife,
the poetry of survival,
a rough draft of us on bended
knee prying open the secret
compartment of hell.

Nags Head, North Carolina

Night,
9:31 pm,
no clouds,
just an abundance of stars
we all gaze at in earnest,
the raw bone silence impossible
to bare so we close our textbook eyes,
the nest of Logger Head turtles
in dubstep with
our washboard dreams.

Nobody's catching anything
off the pier, the hours becoming
a history lesson without end.
The flashlight put away,
suddenly it's a go-cart race,
clumsily they rush past the toll gate.
Unless otherwise noted
all the hatchlings made
it to the fire escape.

Beyond the breaking waves,
beyond what we can see
is the overhanging promises
of an endless ocean.

Mt. Kilimanjaro

*The developed world taught Africans
how to be efficient killers, they taught
them to kill wild animals for pleasure.*

Do we have to saw off a rhino's
horn to save him?
The horn makes a nice ornamental
dagger handle, ground up it cures
all our ills, keeps away evil spirits.

All around us animals are relying
on a phantom limb, a bullet jammed
in the chamber, at Land's end Hemingway
turning in all his firearms to be melted.

The snows of Mt. Kilimanjaro are
from a bygone era, when Livingston
barely heard the song of Solomon,
in the real world each night falling
asleep in Darwin's workshop.

As a child, *Timmy* the gorilla at the zoo
frightened me the most. I tiptoed passed
the lions & leopards out into a courtyard
of sorts where one could buy a bag
of peanuts to feed the elephants.

All the noise in the world is but
a drought, the quiet pacing of a tiger
who knows next to nothing of what
it costs to feed him.

Radio - The Taxi of the Night

The radio is ever vigilant,
on the lookout for commies,
duct tapes us to a chair to make
sure we don't miss *The Mystery Hour.*
Nothing like reports of a crashed ufo,
free fish oil for the first 100 callers
or a mattress sale to get me excited.
It is the radio that searches for our
deep hurt, the faith and genius
of the music that evens the odds.
I just want five minutes
of air time to tell the world
you don't get a prize for finishing
last or for picking up dog poop.

In between looking for the lost piano
in the house and cutting my own hair
so I look somewhat respectable
I've invented the better mouse trap.
It's like casting out reel and rod
onto the clear waters to catch fish,
except this is more fun.
You hear the panic in their voices,
the free meal turning out
to be a deadly carnival ride.
Come by and help me kick
in the basement door—
no telling what's down there.